Introduction to Tai Ch
Tai Chi Short Form 28

1

Wudang Form

6. 白鹤亮翅 White crane spreads its wings

7. 左搂膝拗步 Brush knee and twist step - left side

8. 手挥琵琶 Hands strumming the lute

9. 上步搬拦锤 Step forward, parry and punch

10. 小擒拿手 Catch and hold the hand

11. 右踢腿 Right ridge kick

12. 左打虎式 Strike the tiger – left side

13. 右打虎式 Strike the tiger – right side

14. 左搂膝拗步 Brush knee and twist step - left side

15. 野马分鬃 Part the wild horse's mane

16. 正单鞭 Straight single whip

17. 玉女穿梭 Jade woman works at shuttle

18. 正单鞭 Straight single whip

19. 下势 Push down

20. 上步七星 Step forward with seven stars

21. 退步跨虎 Step back and ride the tiger

22. 双摆莲 Double lotus kick

23. 弯弓射虎 Bend the bow and shoot the tiger

24. 上步搬拦捶 Step forward, parry and punch

25. 如封似闭 Apparent close-up

26. 十字手 Cross hands

27. 抱虎归山 Hold the tiger and return to the mountain

28. 收势 Finishing

Part 1

Introduction

Chapter 1
The Way of Tai Chi

What is Tai chi? Where did it come from and how did it evolve? Tai chi is a series of movements developed over hundreds of years in China. These movements were developed for self defense, health, longevity, and spiritual reasons. These practices embody many traditional roots spanning thousands of years. Over this amount of time tai chi has also developed into many different styles, often emphasizing different goals.

Tai chi: Martial Art, Exercise, Meditation?

For millennia people in India, Nepal, Tibet, China, and throughout Asia have used exercises to improve their health, fight disease, increase vitality, and improve the length and overall quality of life. Over four thousand years these exercises and practices have grown to include stretching, breathing methods, static postures, and herbal remedies. These methods and practices are the root and foundation from which tai chi developed.

Tai chi is a physical practice of movements used for martial arts, health, and spiritual practices. There are texts that use the term tai chi in reference to physical practices dating back as far 100 CE. The term being used as a description of a martial art can be found in a small number of texts as early as 900 CE. Many of these old texts are referring to practices based on using ancient beliefs and techniques or philosophical concepts and principles. Most of these are incomplete or not specific about the practices themselves. The tai chi practices today may include similar principles or philosophies to these early mentions of tai chi, but the many different styles practiced today can only date their roots to as early as the thirteenth/fourteenth century.

Over centuries of development tai chi has branched into many different styles, which differ greatly both in appearance and practice. Tai chi of the same style can also differ between each individual practitioner. Depending on the style or practitioner, the goals of tai chi practice normally include one or more of the following goals: martial arts; health and longevity; mental and spiritual focus or refinement.

Traditionally tai chi was developed and practiced as a martial art. As a result of millennia of conflict and war in Chinese history, as well as the common occurrence of bandits and robbers in the countryside, martial arts pervaded a large part of Chinese culture. So common and widespread was this culture that it even became intertwined with temples and religious sects. China has a long history of martial arts tradition, in which martial arts are divided into 2 categories; internal and external. External martial arts often focus on first training the external, or outside, body first, such as physical strength, skin toughness, iron shirt, etc. From the external practices would over time turn more inward into the mind and relaxation. Many external martial arts have Buddhist roots in China, most well known of which is Shaolin monastery in Hebei province.

Internal martial arts normally begin on training the internal body first through a variety of training including meditation, qigong, breathing exercises, etc. Eventually internal martial arts start to improve and strengthen the external body as well. Tai chi is considered the premier and origin of all internal martial arts of China. Daoist philosophy influenced the development of tai chi in using principles of internal strength with soft, yielding power as opposed to external strength or hard, direct force.

Tai chi focuses on building the internal strength through proper breathing and body alignment, while slowly building up physical external strength, which will be discussed later. Martial arts practices include push hands and application drills. When practiced as a martial art, tai chi focuses on building strength, fighting applications, and sensitivity through two person exercises. By practicing with an emphasis on martial arts, proper technique and form are emphasized as well as breath control. Typically, Chen style tai chi exhibits more of these aspects. Today tai chi is less often practiced as a martial art and has often abandoned many of the full martial practices.

Along with being developed as a martial art, tai chi drew upon the long history of health and spiritual practices common to Daoism. Since fighting and protection were not a constant threat, tai chi also incorporated many Daoist practices to improve health and regulation of the body. In modern times, tai chi has returned to these roots and is commonly practiced for its many health benefits.

Yang Style

The oldest known style of tai chi was practiced by the Chen family. For hundreds of years it was taught only within their family until one day a man by the name of Yang Lu Chan went undercover as a servant in their household to secretly learn their martial art, which later became known as tai chi. This man later created a new lineage or style of tai chi that was only taught within his family and became known as Yang style. It wasn't until the late 19th century that tai chi became well known and taught openly to the public throughout China. A lot of this advancement can be attributed to Yang Cheng Fu.

Yang Cheng Fu (1883 - 1936) became famous at the turn of the 20th century as a martial arts champion. Yang saw the health benefits tai chi could provide all of society, so he modified tai chi and began teaching it publicly. Much of tai chi's fame, popularity, and spread can likely be attributed to Yang Cheng Fu's contributions.

Everyday throughout the world, tai chi can be seen being practiced by a wide array of people of all ages and backgrounds for its myriad of health benefits. Modern science and research is starting to confirm these benefits, which include, but are not limited to, improved circulation, lung capacity, cardiovascular health, and arthritis relief. Tai chi is a low impact form of exercise with very limited risks and due to its versatility it can be suitable for almost any age group. When practiced mainly for health reasons, tai chi is likely to focus on form, alignment, balance, and relaxation. Yang style has historically been linked to advocating and promoting these health aspects, which today continues to emphasize overall health.

The health aspects may be one of the most common goals and aims of modern practice, but these aspects have a long history with spiritual and philosophical schools. Longevity, long life, has been a key part of Daoist theory and practice for thousands of years.

Daoism is a philosophy, belief system, and sometimes a religion that developed from traditional Chinese thought. Daoist philosophy and practices have long been concerned with improving health and longevity through the use of physical and mental exercises. Aside from the previously discussed physical health benefits, tai chi also benefits the mind, Daoists consider mental and spiritual health to be of equal or greater importance than the more physical. Often times improving physical health was done for increasing longevity, which increased the amount of time to work on mental and spiritual development. The practice of tai chi itself is used in the development of mental and spiritual health. Through learning to relax the body and tuning into the breath, the mind also begins to become relaxed. As the mind relaxes it is easier to focus and enter a meditative state. Once a more meditative state is achieved, practice can also start to become more spiritual.

When practiced for mental and spiritual development tai chi practice often focuses on relaxing and developing internal awareness. Martial arts application is often not as important as emphasis on precise movement according to standard form. Wudang Zhang Sanfeng style tai chi focuses much more on the internal health benefits and mental awareness. Internal awareness is practiced to create a strong healthy body and mind leading to a meditative state of being.

As a result of tai chi's long history it has been developed into many different styles. These styles include and emphasize a combination of martial arts, health, and spiritual practices. Different styles may stress or emphasize improving certain aspects over others, but the benefits of tai chi are gained in all. To get the complete benefits of tai chi all aspects should be worked on and improved. All forms of tai chi involve the practices as a direct result of its roots and ties with Daoism.

Section 2

Daoist Roots

The ideas found in tai chi have their roots tied to traditional Chinese thought and Daoist philosophical concepts. The name tai chi itself is taken from key concepts in traditional Chinese thought thousands of years old. Tai chi not only takes the name of a Daoist concept, but also incorporates Daoist concepts of duality (yin and yang), stressing the importance of health into its methodology and practices.

太 极 拳

The name tai chi, which is the abbreviated form of tai chi chuan, is a Romanized translation of the word 太极拳. It can also be translated as tai ji quan, t'ai c'hi ch'uan., and is often simply called tai chi or taiji leaving off the last word.

Tai chi is comprised of two words tai 太 and ji 极 (note: the old method of translating Chinese used to Romanize this word was "chi," the modern system Romanizes it as "ji".) In modern times these words are more commonly pronounced as ji versus chi and for the rest of this section "Taiji" will be used for the Daoist concept, but will continue to use tai chi when referring to the physical practice. Tai means the highest, greatest, excessive, or extreme, while ji 极 means the utmost or the extreme. The last word quan (old system: chuan) 拳 means fist and simply denotes a martial art. For this reason tai chi chuan is sometimes translated as the grand ultimate, or supreme ultimate, fist.

This word is taken directly from the Daoist concept of Taiji which is the balanced, unified whole of everything in existence. Taiji is the highest extremes, represented by the recognizable symbol of a circle half black and half white, Taiji represents the whole, pure, complete, and balanced state of anything and everything.

Tai chi chuan uses this name because it encompasses many Daoist principles with a goal of reaching an internal balance and wholeness. The tai chi symbol itself is often seen with the white and black halves distinctly separated. This distinct separation in Daoism represents duality, or the idea of opposites, such as positive and negative, left and right, often known as yin and yang.

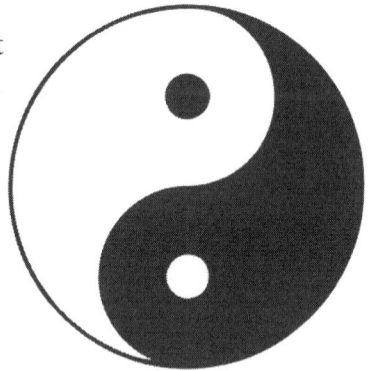

The concept of yin and yang is seen throughout the movements in tai chi, where many moves are done in balance. Hand and arm movements often move in opposite direction creating a balance within the movement. While practicing, take a look at the way your body is moving; left and right, forward and backward motions and movements being done in balance with regard to relaxation, position, and speed.

Inhaling and exhaling also represent different qualities related to yin and yang. During exhale the movement is most likely expanding outward (yang) with the breath and during inhalation the movement or body is receding or retracting (yin) in with the breath. For example, as will be seen in the foundational exercises, shifting the weight or stepping forward is done while exhaling, and inhaling when shifting the weight back or stepping backward. In addition to just external movements, the concept of yin and yang are also applied to the body as a whole internally and externally. While the body is being active and in movement it is being yang, yet if done correctly the mind will become still and focused representing yin.

Yin and Yang

Yin represents the feminine and yang represents the masculine. These concepts reach beyond only one single definition but rather a general idea found in every object and everything.

Yin	Yang	Yin	Yang
cold	hot	spiritual	physical
black	white	contract	expand
internal	external	female	male
moon	sun	negative (-)	positive (+)

Each aspect of the movements coincide primarily with one of these two ideas and concepts, but together they form a unified whole that should be in balance. In Daoism the concept of the two universal pairs of opposite come to a unified balance creating a whole known as Taiji (tai chi). Tai chi as a practice creates balance between outside movement and inner stillness in addition to the unification of the opposing forces in each movement.

These ideas of balance and unification in Daoism and traditional Chinese thought have also had an emphasis on building personal health and increasing longevity. The idea of taiji along with yin and yang are integral to pursuing the overall goals of improving health and longevity. The body in and of itself is considered, as a whole, representative of taiji. It is comprised of yin and yang on a large scale as well as on a small scale. Even though the body is highly complex, each of the individual parts contain an amount of yin and yang. Daoist practices, including tai chi, aim to find a natural balance of those qualities in each part of the body, and eventually for the body as a whole. When the body finds balance it not only becomes healthier, but also stronger and more efficient. This balance is also a key to helping increase the lifespan and quality of life. While improved health and increased longevity are important to many people, regardless of philosophical disposition, they are a key elements found in Daoism that have been cultivated throughout China over thousands of years.

While all styles of tai chi come from Daoism and are said to come from Wudang itself, Daoist thought is paramount in Wudang Zhang Sanfeng tai chi, due to the fact of its continual development in the secluded mountain temples. All forms and styles of tai chi share their roots and origins in Daoism. Despite the varying stories of tai chi's creation and the differences between styles, they all contain and employ Daoist philosophy and concepts.

Legends and Lineages

Tai chi has roots that date back thousands of years, but many of those roots are only similar in ideas and concepts, rather than in actual practices. Tai chi similar to the form as it is known today has legends and lineages that have developed in the past thousand years. The oldest and most uninterrupted lineage of tai chi practitioners today is the Chen family style, yet stories of earlier practitioners or practices still exist. The legends and stories of tai chi's origins as a physical practice begin in the Wudang mountains nearly a thousand years ago, but recorded history can only trace roots back a few hundred years. Tai chi's evolution from traditional roots, to the legends of Zhang Sanfeng, and the more modern styles of the Chen and Yang family, have all influenced the tai chi that is practiced today.

Daoism is found throughout China, but in the past many temples were often established in more secluded areas surrounded by nature. There are five "holy" mountains in China known for their temples and roles as homes of personal or spiritual cultivation. One of these great mountains is known as Wudang (also translated as wutang, wutan, or wudan), which is the legendary birthplace of tai chi.

The Wudang Mountains (wudangshan 武当山) have been a renowned center for academics related to Daoism, traditional medicine, meditation, health exercises, and internal martial arts since at least 700 CE. These mountains are primarily located in Hubei province in central China, and have also been a haven for Daoists and internal cultivators, the most well known of which was the legendary martial artist Zhang Sanfeng, creator of tai chi.

Zhang Sanfeng (张三丰), sometimes translated as Chang San Feng, is disputed whether or not to have existed at all, or is a composite of more than one person whose story and reputation have reached somewhat mythical proportions. With the information that is available it is believed that Zhang San Feng lived during the 13th century. He is reported to have lived to be 200 years old (1247-1447 CE), but his date of death is uncertain. If these claims were to be true he would have lived during the Song, Yuan, and Ming dynasties.

According to legends, Zhang San Feng originally trained and studied at the Shaolin Buddhist Monastery in Henan Province. After years of study Zhang left the hard physical practices of the Chan Buddhists and traveled to study the softer internal arts in the Daoist temples of Wudang Mountain. While studying the soft, yielding principles in Daoist philosophy he drew upon his observations of the nature around him and found inspiration for bringing together these principles with his martial arts knowledge.

As early as 1670 it was written in Epitaph for Wang Zhengnan by Huang Zongxi that Zhang Sanfeng was the founder of internal martial arts. Most stories of Zhang recount of an encounter one day while out on a walk in the woods, involving a bird (often a crane or a magpie) and a snake. Zhang observed the two fighting, noticing the soft, supple, relaxed movements the snake made as the bird tried to strike directly at it. The snake yielded from the attacks using these soft and supple movements, while it skillfully took focus and struck back at the crane. The bird too contained its own useful characteristics in sharp and direct attacks in contrast to that of the snake. This fight is said to be the inspiration for Zhang creating an internal martial art, incorporating the movements with his understanding of Daoist

The fight that inspired Zhang Sanfeng, depicted with a crane.

principles and fighting techniques. The movements and natural techniques of the snake represented the soft, yin, side that is most characteristic of tai chi movements. Each animal not only exhibited purely yin or yang, some of the snakes movements were yang in directness and focus, while the crane too had complementary yin aspects of evasion.

Previously most other martial arts, including those practiced by Buddhists monks, initially focused on training hard physical exterior strength. Zhang took the opposite approach and focused training on internal awareness of the breath and body to develop core power while maintaining relaxation and suppleness throughout the body.

Over the next several hundred years his style was closely guarded and only passed down to one or two people each generation. The history and lineage of tai chi was lost for generations and is at current speculative. Later legends claim that a man by the name Wang Zongyue had learned an early form of tai chi under the lineage of Zhang Sanfeng and was the teacher of Chen Wang Ting. Chen Wang Ting (1580-1660) is the founder of Chen style tai chi, which some speculate or assert is the real origin of what would become tai chi. Most of the major and most well known styles of tai chi today can trace their roots to Chen village, home of the Chen family and their internal martial arts.

Today there are many different styles of tai chi that have developed over the past several hundred years, most notable systems are Chen and Yang systems. These systems have the most histories and complete lineages. The Chen family tai chi is the oldest and has the longest uninterrupted lineage of tai chi, any lineage or teachings that predate them is speculative or considered as legends by modern day scholars.

As mentioned earlier Yang style tai chi was created by Yang Lu Chan. Yang Lu Chan had learned the style by secretly studying the Chen family martial arts system, although at the time it was not known as or called tai chi. Yang Lu Chan sold all his belongings and went undercover as a servant in the Chen household for the sole purpose of secretly watching and studying their style of martial arts. Yang was only discovered when he came to meet a fight challenge delivered to the Chen family. No Chen family members were available, willing or able to meet the challenge and so Yang accepted it. Yang won the fight with ease using the Chen family system to win. Yang then developed Yang family style tai chi that later became the style that helped tai chi greatly spread publicly as well as being the foundation of modernized or standardized tai chi.

The stories of Zhang Sanfeng creating an internal martial art based around Daoism and having passed it on to Wang Zongyue may not be anything more than myth. These stories may have been added to create a more colorful history and background, but at the very least they provide insight and embody the fundamental ideas of Daoism that tai chi are based on.

Scholars and modern research have been able to clearly trace the creation of tai chi to the internal martial arts practiced and developed by the Chen family in the 1600's. The Yang family further developed these internal arts into what became known as tai chi. Both styles still exist today and have spawned many other styles.

Tai chi is not easily defined as any one single thing because it contains many different aspects. The many differing styles that have evolved often contain elements of the same roots and goals. Although these goals may be different they were developed and created from traditional Chinese ideas. The concepts come from Daoist thought and philosophy of yin and yang. Throughout history and continuing to modern times tai chi has been practiced as a means of self defense, health improvement, and spiritual cultivation. These aspects can all be practiced to varying degrees and the intensity of focus is dependent on the style and individual. Even with the wide range of practices and diversity amongst tai chi practitioners, certain similarities between all styles are seen from their shared roots.

Chapter 2
The Art of Tai Chi

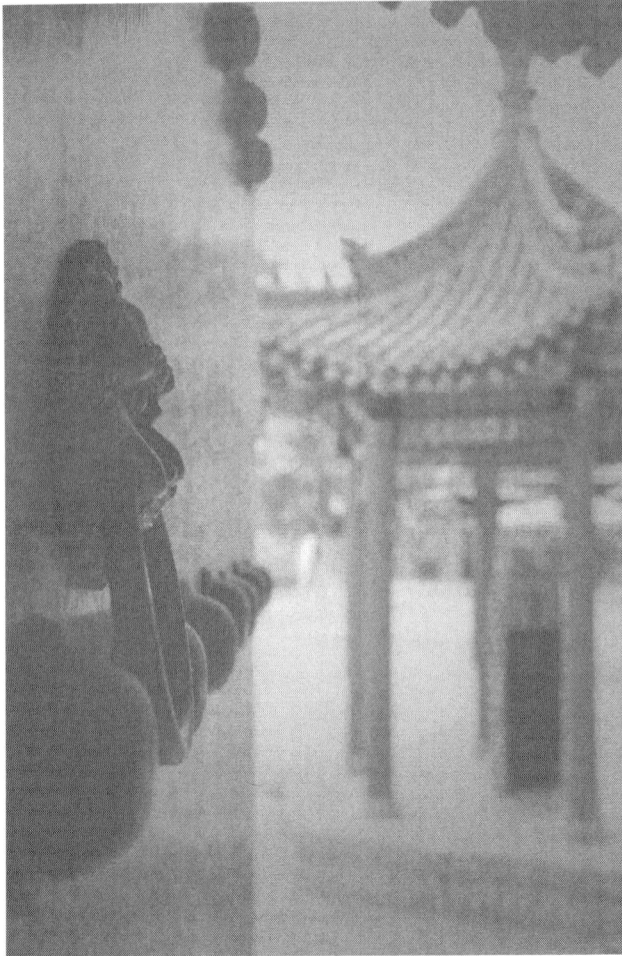

Each style of tai chi has its unique characteristics that come from different goals, developed over hundreds of years, yet some general characteristics are found in most styles. These characteristics can be seen in outside physical movements, felt in the internal benefits throughout the body system, and experienced in the mental focus.

Section 1

External Characteristics

Common characteristics can be seen in the physical movements and body positions throughout the variety of tai chi styles. Although each individual move in tai chi can vary between individual practitioners and is distinctly different from other movements, there are still many shared characteristics. Common physical characteristics may include a rounded body posture, circular movements, and all done in a slow controlled manner.

Tai chi stresses keeping a strong posture with a straight back, yet the body maintains a rounded appearance, especially in the upper body. As the practitioner learns to achieve physical relaxation in all parts of the body, it will naturally become more round. Example of rounded posture from tai chi form is evident in the movement Ride the Tiger.

The relaxation that causes the rounded postures should be practiced and developed not only in the muscles, but also the skeletal system. The round appearance in the arms and legs are caused by keeping the joints relaxed and unlocked. The knees and elbows retain a slight bend throughout each movement. Even while maintaining a straight back the upper body still becomes rounded as the shoulders relax, falling slightly forward while the chest sinks down and inward. The postures and position of the body keep the rounded appearance as a result of this relaxation throughout the body and it is retained by the characteristic of movements and transitions between positions in a circular and twisting nature.

In addition to the body and limbs having a rounded

position, the movements themselves exhibit circular characteristics. Accentuated by the relaxed limbs many arm movements rotate from and to various positions, often times the hands will rotate with each other as if rotating a ball. (See foundation exercise #4)

The circular characteristics of tai chi movements extend beyond just the body posture and the movements of the upper limbs to incorporate the rest of the body. As many techniques are practiced at a variety of angles, most transitions involve turning and rotating achieved through the movements of the waist and lower body. The development of using circular movements throughout techniques can be attributed to a number of interrelated reasons. These reasons include the aforementioned relaxation, continuous movement, and balance between opposing forces within the movements.

Relaxation and the idea of a constant flow between opposing forces affect the physical aspect of the movements the most. Relaxation gives the body a state and condition which it is trying to maintain in any given position, as well as during the interconnected movements.

In order to minimize the loss of energy or excessive use of energy, tai chi practice often changes directions gradually, rather than abruptly, through redirecting energy or force between directions. This gradual redirecting is done most effectively when

---

70 % rule

As a result of the idea of conserving energy, Zhang Sanfeng tai chi has a general rule of only doing things to about 70% of maximum.

While this number is not a strict number, it is to remind one of the idea that in practice to not use too much energy. Going a hundred percent often leads to unneeded strain and the possibility of injuries. For strengthening, the body and movement are going far enough to engage the muscles and other viscera while still remaining relaxed.

the body is in a state of relaxation. The use of opposing forces and slowly changing or flowing between them while maintaining a relaxed body are the root for the development of circular movements.

If there is a force or something coming directly at you to try and stop it takes a lot of energy and the force of impact can be felt. Tai chi aims to not try and abruptly stop that kind of force but to redirect it, which is done through circular movements. To switch directions abruptly causes the original energy to be stopped and lost before a new force needs to be generated in the new direction.

Probably the most well known and often the most visibly noticeable characteristic of tai chi is the use of slow, controlled, and fluid movements. The slowness is achieved by learning to link each individual movement with the breath. During each inhalation and exhalation a different movement is performed. Tai chi stresses taking long, deep, slow, and equal length breaths.

As a result of greater breath control along with being linked with movement, tai chi is practiced in a slow, smooth, controlled manner. While the movements are connected to the breath, tai chi is also practiced at the slow rate for a number of other reasons. It allows for better energy conservation, proper technique, a relaxed state, and heightening awareness throughout the body and its connections.

All of these physical characteristics provide the body with a variety of health benefits. The legs and lower body in particular are strengthened by these slow movements and the occasional one legged positions. Overall coordination increases, while muscle and respiratory endurance increases. Bone density is increased due to sustained skeletal pressure. Relaxation in the muscles and joints through movement is the basic physical characteristics of tai chi that continues to be developed and emphasized more and more through practice. When all parts of the body are relaxed, the limbs and outer joints are not straightened or made stiff, nor extended to their maximum. The body does not make sharp, rigid, or jerky movements when the body is relaxed.

No matter what style of tai chi, the characteristics of rounded postures, circular movements, and slow controlled movements will be present as the result of the common practices of total relaxation of muscles and joints in gentle circular movements in conjunction with the breath. These external characteristics are deeply influenced by the practice of relaxation which is also a key in influencing the internal and mental characteristics.

Internal Characteristics

Aside from the visible physical characteristics, tai chi also has several distinctive characteristics internally. The lungs, heart, and internal systems are all regulated while being stimulated in healthy ways. Tai chi helps to strengthen the internal body systems through a combination of active awareness and passive development. The early stages of learning tai chi begins with control and awareness of the breath, often through qi gong or breathing exercises. These breathing techniques help to affect the heart and circulatory system. Overall tai chi internally conditions and strengthens the respiratory system, the heart and circulatory system, all while developing a deeper internal awareness into other parts of the body.

The respiratory system, namely the use of the lungs and breathing are the foundation of tai chi and one of the easiest places to start to become internally aware. Breathing is an easy first step because it is an internal function that, to some extent, we have control over on a frequent basis (e.g. holding the breath, deep breathing, rapid breathing, etc.) Tai chi involves taking long, slow, deep breaths with equal inhalation and exhalation.

Deep breathing helps with the entire body in blood oxygenation and lung capacity. Understanding, awareness, and control of the breath is of special importance in tai chi as it is closely linked to movement. Specific breathing techniques will be discussed in depth in Chapter 4. Different styles of tai chi all practice some form of breath control and deep breathing, all leading to tai chi practitioners to have more even breath flow and increased lung capacity. As tai chi is practiced longer and over a long period, the core, diaphragm, and lungs are strengthened from the constant practice of specific breathing techniques.

From the use of different breathing techniques used in tai chi the rest of the body begins to be affected and improve. The heart and circulatory systems may not be discussed as often or directly as breathing and the respiratory system, yet all styles of tai chi share the characteristic of improving the cardiac system in a variety of ways. The heart and circulatory system experience improvement in a short period of time after utilizing Daoist breathing techniques. Research has shown that the heart rate and blood pressure often begins to lower in only a matter of weeks of starting a regular tai chi regimen. When breathing is done in a slow controlled deep manner, it allows the blood to absorb more oxygen into and discard more carbon dioxide out of the blood system. The heart rate lowers as it needs to pump less blood throughout the body, because the blood contains more oxygen. In addition to lowering the heart rate, there is evidence that cholesterol levels are also lowered. Even though tai chi is performed slowly it is still considered an aerobic exercise. The rest of the circulatory system also improves along with the strength of the heart, part of this is due to an increased relaxation of muscles allowing smoother blood flow. For example, think about when in a stressed situation or when panicked, we are often told to take deep breath to help calm down, we calm down as a result of this extra oxygen and the heart rate lowering.

The affects of tai chi expand beyond the respiratory and circulatory systems to eventually develop a greater awareness of the body overall. Initially felt through deep internal relaxation, awareness of different types of activity in the body begin being felt, many times with the eventual goal of awareness and control of individual internal systems and organs. As discussed with the physical characteristics relaxation is a common and important characteristic externally in tai chi, but it is equally, if not more, important as an internal characteristic. From the muscles learning to relax, the relaxation goes deeper into the body; the joints and connective tissue (a result and contributor to the rounded postures). This relaxation is often then continued deeper into the body and the organs, which can happen naturally or worked on through conscious effort.

The combination of the way in which breath work is done, along with the circular movements in the limbs, and twisting of the torso, the internal organs are constantly being massaged. While breathing with focus on the diaphragm and movement of muscles of the ribcage are engaged and slowly controlled building their strength while increasing awareness of their function. Along with the developed sense of the different regulatory systems and processes in the body eventually this internal awareness can grow into a deeper understanding of any organs involved in these processes. This is considered a much higher and more difficult level of awareness to achieve, but most tai chi does aim to develop awareness at the most minute levels to help benefit in some way.

Although internal awareness and development is in and of itself a main characteristic in all tai chi styles, their development can be practiced, taught and progress in a vast number of ways. The result of a combination of the physical characteristics along with breathing practices, internal awareness will become heightened. An example of this awareness is the common sensation of heat and warmth developing in the hands. This is a result of many things including relaxation and an increase in circulation, which increases heat, as well as heightened sensitivity to feel these small changes. While the degree of and which type of sensitivity developed may vary from one style to another, they all share the characteristic of developing a heightened sense of awareness to different internal systems, especially breathing and blood flow.

The mind too begins to take a role in the internal as well, while the mind itself is part of the internal, the mind can aid in raising internal awareness in other parts of the body. As the mind begins to become focused more through mental and spiritual practices, its ability to focus and control increases. When the mind is no longer thinking of random thoughts or ideas, the background chatter goes away, at that point the mind can then begin to focus on feeling the sensitivity of the internal organs.

Mental Characteristics

While the mind is a part of internal characteristics, it is also important to view it as a separate and equally important point of focus in training. All tai chi shares the characteristic that the mind is a key and distinct part of proper training. The training of the mind, along with spiritual goals are commonly found and trained at more advanced levels of tai chi practice. Building mental control and awareness is often, but not always, used as a precursor toward spiritual practices. Sometimes this focus may be on a specific intent, energy awareness, or meditative in nature. In tai chi the mind is focused using several techniques leading to meditation, which, along with other characteristics, benefit the brain and mental health. Tai chi begins by learning about mental focus and mental awareness, often through a variety of supplementary exercises, sometimes leading towards specific spiritual goals.

Focusing the mind is common in all tai chi, although the exact way to focus the mind may be different. Common elements exist between the styles often seen as a direct and indirect result of this mental focusing. All tai chi focuses the mind on something, regardless of what the focus is, the result of reaching a state of focus is a key characteristic. This focus is the foundation of awareness and regulation of the entire body, while the mind also becomes more self-aware. The development of these aspects normally begins with mental focus that aid in meditation. The practice of tai chi itself is a form of mental focus. Mental focus is a key to being able to succeed in meditation. The initial goal is to begin slowing down the chatter and thoughts in the mind.

Many traditions use allegories or metaphors to describe the mind and the seemingly endless flow of thoughts. One such metaphor is that the mind is like a horse running wild. The horse (mind) needs to first be tethered (focused) to something in order to calm done. The mind can focus on anything simple to achieve a quieter, calmer mind. Commonly the breath is used as a focal point in meditations from different backgrounds such as Yoga, Buddhism, Daoism, etc. As the mind focuses on any or all of those aspects it will start to ignore and, eventually, cease to have as many random thoughts. With regular practice it becomes easier to achieve greater mental focus quicker and deeper through mental relaxation.

All tai chi styles not only develop mental focus passively, but often actively through additional practices, including meditation. Although the definition of meditation is unclear and differs from practice or tradition, it normally come from a heightened state of self awareness through focus. Tai chi itself can become a form of focus, but due to its complex movements can initially be difficult, for this reason many systems employ supplemental practices to solely help develop mental awareness.

The most common forms and well known types of meditation in varying practices are stationary and involve little to no movement. Sitting or standing still meditations are often taught in conjunction with tai chi. In these positions the inhale and exhale are focused upon to help still the mind. The lack of movement helps limit the amount of outside stimulus that can be distracting.

Other exercises regularly include "qigong", or energy work exercises. These exercises can have a variety of movements and purposes depending on the style of tai chi, but they almost all include focusing the mind while doing a limited amount of movements. These exercises will include more static postures that are held for a short period of time, much more similar to sequences of different body postures as found in Hatha Yoga. These exercises all help to introduce body movement into practice while still keeping the mind focused. These practices help bridge the gap of still meditation, as many people are used to, into moving meditation.

All tai chi has the capability to reach a meditative state while moving. Initially the mind is focused on just trying to remember the movement and the order while trying to correct them. Focusing on these many aspects does not allow the mind to reach a heightened state of awareness or clarity, but after each movement has been practiced regularly, the mind needs to think less about the movement and begin to focus on itself. The mind quiets by focusing on the movement and breath, then as those foci disappear the mind becomes even more quiet and tranquil.

Each movement in tai chi is done with slow movements in coordination with the breath; this allows the mind to focus on not only the breath, but also the precision and relaxation within the movement. The initial steps of practice involve simply letting the relaxation of body and breath in movement to also continue into the mind. As body and breath become unified, so do the thoughts of the mind. The act of unifying the mind on a single point, or concentrating, is the first step towards meditation. Through consistent and regular practice a meditative state can be reached while in motion. It is this development that is the reason why tai chi itself can be used as a form of meditation and sometimes referred to as meditation in motion.

Meditation is often associated with a specific spiritual

system or goal. As a result of tai chi's history, creation, and background with Daoist philosophy, many of the characteristics in physical movements, breath work, and mental focus discussed above are related to the philosophies and spiritual ideas of balance and simplicity. The ideas and philosophies found in Daoism were used to create tai chi and are inseparable from the art. The movements of tai chi are used to create a balance of internal and external, finding balance in both strength and relaxation.

Creating balance and harmony internally while emptying the mind is a direct representation of the Daoist idea of balancing Yin and Yang. As relaxation and awareness both reach a deep level, the mind eventually relaxes. When discussing the goals of tai chi these are seen in the practices of regulation of the mind and spirit as later goals. Focusing the mind while developing into meditation works to strengthen the ability of emptying the mind. In traditional Daoist philosophy the concept of emptiness (无极) is important and plays a key role in the creation of Taiji (which remember from Chapter 1 is where the name tai chi comes from.) In tai chi practice the empty state of mind is a later goal and higher state to be developed, which will be discussed in later books. Another goal in spiritual development amongst Daoists is longevity, or the increase in the individuals lifespan. Longevity is still a major role in all forms of tai chi through its aim towards improved physical and mental health. Through meditation and mental focus these goals of longevity can be aided and achieved because they help to reduce stress.

Even if the spiritual practices or goals aren't there, many Daoist ideas and concepts still exist in the mental exercises of many styles of tai chi. These practices may differ in their specific goals, but for the mind they all help to develop focus and relaxation, which all share similar benefits of greater mental balance, internal balance, stress relief, mental focus and relaxation. The body also benefits in improved chemical, hormonal, and internal systems function, regulation, and balance.

Wudang Zhang Sanfeng tai chi is very closely related to the ideas of their Daoist roots and thus influences their goals and aims in this practice. These goals in Wudang tai chi involve finding a state of emptiness and finding a natural balance and efficiency within oneself as well as with the external world. Utilizing key ideas and concepts of Daoism in the practice of tai chi all help in the practices of meditation in motion.

The External, Internal, and Mental Characteristics

Overall tai chi can be approached from a variety of ways and practiced with different goals with individual intents. Traditionally created as a martial arts, its roots in Daoism allowed it to also be practiced spiritually and philosophically, today it is mostly practiced for its wide range of health benefits for the entire body and mind.

All the different forms of tai chi and approaches to tai chi practice share many characteristics on a physical, internal, and mental level. External physical characteristics of relaxed, circular, and slow movements become connected to the breath, building internal awareness of circulation and the nervous system, which help develop a peace and clarity of mind. Deep relaxation and development of internal awareness are unique and core to what makes any tai chi the internal art it is known as. Advanced and more subtle characteristics of tai chi practice involve mental focus to the point of reaching a type of meditation. This state of meditation helps the mind find balance, which sometimes is practiced as one of many exercises as part of reaching a larger spiritual goal.

These characteristics are not separate from each other, rather they interact and influence one another as tai chi is practiced. Tai chi utilizes slow movements in order to help focus on breathing and correct posture. As the mind slows down the movements become more fluid and relaxed allowing the breath to slow, which helps the mind focus and quiet.

Tai chi aims to regulate the body, breath, mind, qi, and spirit. Through building internal awareness the individual can gain the ability to regulate these things. It is from these practices that tai chi builds and strengthens the body providing a variety of health benefits.

Part 2

Developing Awareness

Chapter 3
Body Awareness

Stability * Alignment * Relaxation

How aware of your body are you?

Are the muscles relaxed? the joints? tendons? ligaments?

Is the body in good alignment? Spine straight or curved?

Where is the center of gravity? the majority of the body weight?

Are the feet and base of the body stable?

Is body weight and position balanced? overextended?

Being one of the first aspects of practice learned, building awareness of the body is an important part of tai chi. Body movement can be simple enough to make it an easy starting place, yet complex enough that even at later stages it is continually being understood and refined. Building awareness of the body can come about in a number of ways; simply being more physically active builds awareness naturally of all the parts being used. Tai chi, with its slow movements, gives the mind time to spend becoming aware of the body as a whole, instead of focusing only on an individual part. This awareness helps the body to refine its movements and positions to be more efficient, safer, healthier, and more relaxed.

Practicing tai chi builds awareness of the body. Building awareness in the body can start from a number of places and emphasized differently depending on perceived importance, but no matter the approach, key elements are important to this awareness. All forms of tai chi emphasize a strong base or stance with correct body alignment. From those foundations relaxation becomes more prevalent and through this relaxation a heightened sensitivity emerges allowing for improved body regulation. Whole body awareness begins with building overall stability through the lower body, maintaining good posture, and learning to release physical tension throughout the body.

Stability

The lower body acts as the foundation for the entire body, it is important in maintaining stability through each movement. To help understand how the lower body interacts in movement efficiently, first look at the basic mechanics involved. Beginning by looking at the physical placement of the legs to create stability in different positions, then examine how the rest of the body interacts with the base in movement while not overextending.

The lower body is concerned with the placement of the feet, legs and pelvis. Focusing on the structure and position of each of these components is used to create a strong base or stance. With overall proper alignment, while sinking the weight towards the hips, a stronger foundation will develop. Like the roots of a tree the weight and energy should feel as if it is pushing into the ground and outward. In Chinese martial arts and tai chi alike, this feeling is often referred to as rooting, which is a common term used to describe the strength and stability in connection with the ground in any given stance or position. (This is an oversimplification of the concept of rooting, which will be discussed in greater detail in Book 2: Intermediate Tai chi.) The feet should both feel firm on the ground connected and pushing or engaging into the floor.

The majority of the body's weight is in the torso and the upper body, which rest on the pelvis. The weight is then distributed from the pelvis into the two legs in equal or non-equal amounts down to the

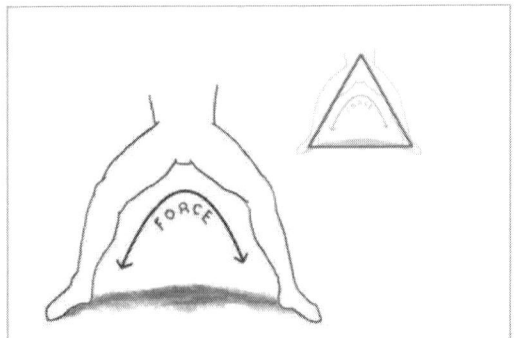

Foundation Weight distribution

ground. Tai chi practice constantly uses movements to help build strength and stability in the lower body. Awareness is built over time from moving from one stance to another.

To understand how this rooting applies and is seen throughout tai chi, as well as many Chinese arts is to look at their common stances. The most common one found in all tai chi and Chinese martial arts is the horse stance.

Horse Stance 马步

This stance is named Horse stance because the final position is similar to that when riding a horse

To practice: place the feet about double shoulder width apart, keeping the feet parallel and pointing forward

Note: This can be done with feet at a variety of different widths apart.

Horse stance develops proper alignment between the hips, knees and feet, while strengthening the leg muscles. Horse stance is a very stable position that is often used in many tai chi standing positions and tai chi exercises because it helps to understand alignment and build awareness in the position of the lower body when the weight is evenly distributed between the legs.

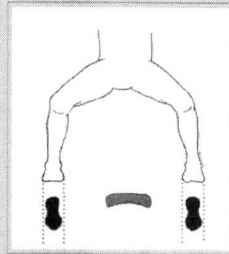

Horse stance

The same principles in creating a strong stance are applied throughout all movements, but this base is only one of several factors in overall stability and balance.

Tai chi also puts a lot of emphasis on coming to an understanding of one's weight, weight distribution and the center of gravity (CoG). This understanding of one's weight is a vital step in beginning to be aware of the body as a whole through stability, balance, and movement.

While many things affect the CoG, the base on which it rides and rests directly affects the movement of the CoG. Often times the pelvis and weight will rest between the legs, sinking low with the feet firmly into the ground. The weight should sink into the legs and ground, avoid raising the body upward or the heels off the ground. A lower center of gravity provides more stability because more body weight is distributed lower, closer to the pelvis. The closer that the majority of your body weight is to the pelvis (top of the base), the more stable the body is. The weight in the upper body should be brought lower towards the pelvis. To avoid raising the center of gravity away from the pelvis, the shoulders and arms should remain relaxed, the chest sunk and hollow, and the breath should be expanding in the abdomen and not the chest.

Just having a lower center of gravity is not enough on its own to create a strong, stable, firm, rooted stance. Depending on where and how an individual is standing can significantly change where their center of gravity is distributed between each leg. Different tai chi styles may emphasis different weight distributions, but all styles develop an understanding of their weight and keeping a lower center of gravity to improve stability while

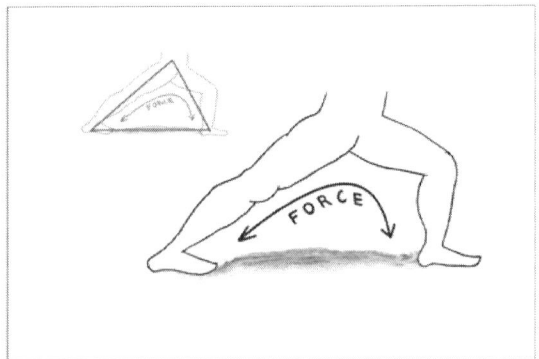

Foundation weight distribution of 30-70 percent

avoiding overextending.

One of the key difficulties or risks while constantly moving is overextending the body or CoG and losing balance. Overextending is the result when the center of gravity is no longer positioned properly in relation to the lower body or the base itself is not stable.

A common mistake found in the aforementioned bow and arrow stance is overextending the knee. A good way of gauging if you are overextending when shifting more weight onto one leg or another is to see where the knee is in correlation to the foot.

An example of this is seen in the bow and arrow stance,

Bow Stance 弓步

The exact translation of this stance is Bow stance, sometimes called a bow and arrow stance, because this is the position archers used to take when shooting:

Begin with the feet at least shoulder width apart up to as much as double shoulder width apart. Turn the body and legs 90 degrees to the left or right so that the hips and shoulders are square. Point both feet at a 45 degree angle in the same direction. Then shift the weight forward bending the leg in front, up to 90 degrees if feet are long enough apart, and allow the back leg to straighten. The weight should be around 70 percent forward. This can be done on either left or right side.

Like all stances they can be done at whatever height or feet distance that is comfortable. Most important is not to push and try to go too low or too far forward.

The position of the front leg partially protects the groin, while more power can be generated for striking by pushing the rear leg into the ground.

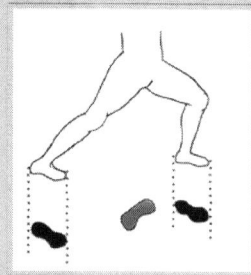

Bow Stance

which is also one the most common in Chinese martial arts, in which the weight is distributed around 70 percent onto one leg and only 30 percent to the other.

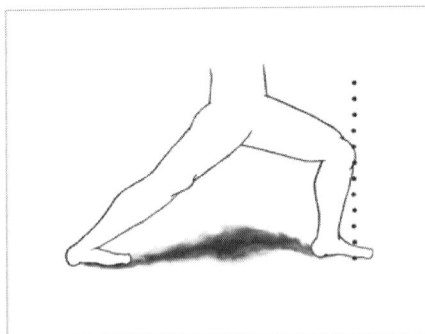

The knee should not extend too far forward

Knee placement in this stance is important to be aware of in order to avoid injuries due to excessive stress caused by overextending. Overextending your weight past the knee is a problem with not keeping the center in balance when shifting the weight in and out of the bow stance.

The knee should not pass the point directly above the foot at about an inch behind the second toe. This point is sometimes referred to as the bubbling spring, in traditional Chinese culture this point is named yongquan 涌泉.

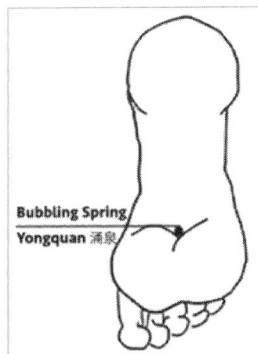

Point of Bubbling Spring

Building a good base by understanding basic alignment in the lower body and how it connects to the center of gravity will help greatly in the natural progression of learning tai chi. Understanding the horse stance and bow stance are important because they are the most common stances that tai chi uses and moves through. By learning to create a strong foundation in these stances the body weight and movement will become more stable and fluid. These foundations serve to hold and carry the weight of the upper body. The connection between the upper and lower body also relies on understanding structure and alignment of the torso.

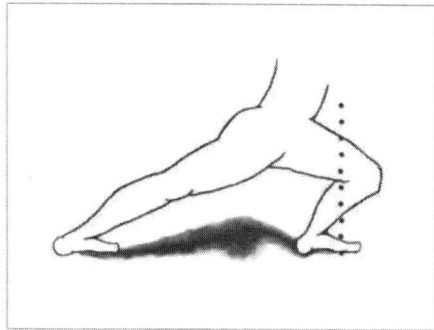

Over extending the knee should be avoided

Section 2

Alignment

While the base of the body and its alignment are important, it still is only a base for which the upper body rests. The upper body contains the core of the body weight, while being connected and controlled by the spine. The most important alignment in any movement, whether it is in tai chi or another activity, is that of the spine. In general the spine should be kept in relatively straight vertical alignment throughout most tai chi movements.

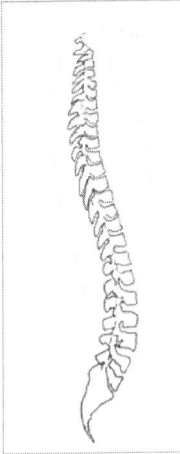

Natural spinal curves

Being conscious of the spine and keeping it straight in every single movement can be a difficult and daunting task. It is easier to first learn to feel what a straight back feels like in a stationary position and as the spine along with the surrounding muscles gets stronger and used to being in that position it will naturally feel more comfortable. Eventually the body will unconsciously start to correct spinal alignment throughout the movements practiced in tai chi.

There are three main areas of focus in the back that are straightened in practice. These three spots coincide with the natural curves in the lower spine, mid back, and neck. In tai chi the back is straightened, but not made fully straight, some of the natural curves of the back still remain. Each of these sections has its own difficulties and unique techniques for aiding in straightening the spine and getting it into proper alignment. Building this foundational awareness begins

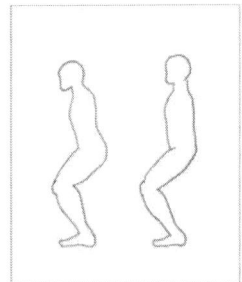

Practice straightening the spine in a standing position

with learning how to get your spine in proper alignment simply while standing.

When initially trying to focus on and straighten these sections, it is easiest to practice while standing in a stationary position. Standing with the feet shoulder width apart, keep the toes pointing forward with the hips and shoulders also facing forward, the body can remain relaxed while working on each section of the spine. Keep a slight bend in the knees and the arms relaxed at the side, while focusing on straightening the spine. Begin by relaxing the spine at the bottom and then working the way up as if building the structure of a building from the ground up. Once relaxed begin focusing on straightening the spine beginning from the bottom.

Lower spine: Tilting the hips.

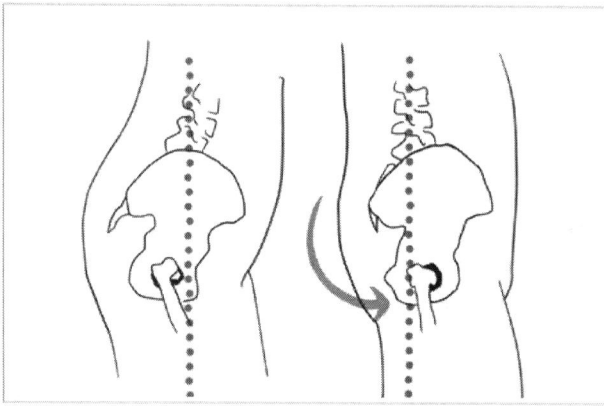

To straighten the lower spine, tuck the hips by rotating the pelvis.

The lower spine is often made straighter than a natural curve, especially in standing or stationary postures. There are a variety of reasons related to meditation and energy work as to why the lower spine should be straightened this much, these reasons will be discussed more in Book 2: Intermediate tai chi. The importance in the initial stages of straightening the lower spine is to focus primarily on the coccyx. The main way that this is achieved is by tilting the pelvis. Through a variety of muscles the pelvis is connected to the spine By tilting the pelvis it allows the psoas and other lower back muscles to relax, which also helps the lower back to straighten.

To achieve this straightened section the pelvis needs to be tilted upward. If having trouble, this can be achieved by sticking the rear out and then tucking in the hips.

By tilting the pelvis and folding in the hips, the lower back will be straightened. Keeping the knees bent will help, and eventually the goal is to be able to relax the lower back muscles in this position.

Mid/upper back: Tucking the ribs

From the lower curve continuing up to the middle back and thoracic region, the back should be straightened to a relaxed degree, while still allowing for some natural curve. Straightening the mid and upper back is the straightening of the thoracic curve. This can often be achieved by standing straight and tall then allowing the body to relax downward with the shoulders slightly forward.

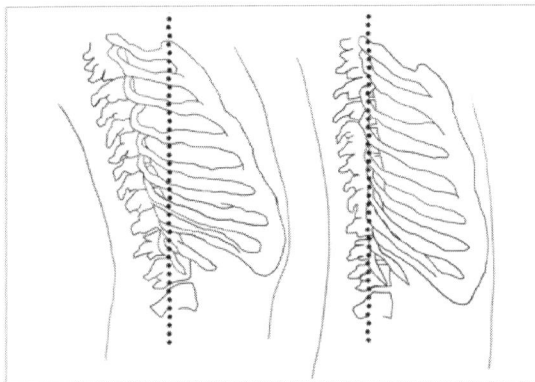

Standing straight involves tucking the ribs (right) and preventing the lower ribs to jut out

When trying to stand straight this curve is sometimes accentuated by a lifting of the chest. When consciously thinking about standing taller and straight the body can have a tendency to overcompensate by expanding the chest outward, increasing the stress on the spine while accentuating its curvature. To correct this problem begin by making sure that the shoulders are relaxed forward and not being stretched or pulled up or back. If the chest is still expanding and/or the mid back is not straight, it will often be noticeable by the lower ribs jutting out and forward.

If this is happening try to lightly tuck in the lower ribs, which will cause the chest cavity to tilt slightly downward. This slight tilt and tucking of the rib cage will straighten out the mid and upper back. Tai chi practitioners, for a variety of reasons, talk about sinking the chest, which helps to alleviate or eliminate the jutting out of the ribs or an over curving of the mid back. Although there is a risk of sinking too much and creating a hunch back, which is also undesired.

Neck: Shifting the head

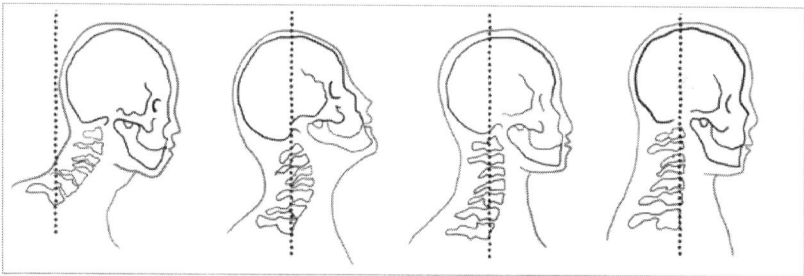

The neck in a variety of positions, slouching or hunchbacked (far left), tilted head (second from left), neck in a normal and a healthy position (second from the right), straightened neck often used in Daoist practices (far right)

The third and final curve in the spine that needs to be straightened out is the cervical region of the neck. This part needs to be straightened by pushing or shifting the head back without tilting it.
One method to help achieve this is to imagine a string connecting

49

at the top of your head, gently pulling upward straightening the spine. Feel the neck being elongated. Once the feeling that the neck is elongated and straight, then relax, allowing the head to come down slightly sitting at the top of the spine. This can help to align the entire spine as well.

Another method is to shift the head back bringing the chin to the neck without tilting the head by looking up or downward. Once in this position then relax the neck and head slightly, this should leave the neck and upper back in a straight alignment.

Drop Stance 仆步

This stance is seen in moves like Push Down.

This stance is often started with the legs nearly double shoulder width apart. While keeping the back straight and the hips facing square with the shoulders, shift the weight mostly onto one leg and then lower the body. In this position, squat on one leg until the thigh is parallel to the ground and extend the other leg out to the side. Both feet are parallel and pointing forward, relative to the torso.

This helps to open the hip flexors and increase flexibility in the legs. Strengthens the legs by having weight mostly on one leg squatting.

Problems that often occur when trying to do this stance involve not being able to go low enough or that the heel wants to come off the ground. The best way to deal with these is to do one of the variations not to strain and slowly build up the flexibility and strength.

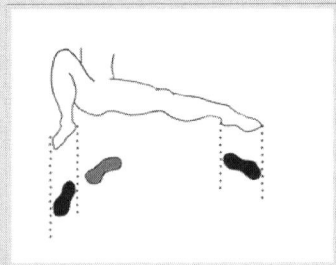

Drop stance

After understanding proper alignment of the spine in a standing position, then one can begin to understand the general spine position found throughout movement. In the standing method just described the spine is in the straightest possible position to help feel the body relax while evenly distributing the body weight downward. During tai chi practice, the spine is not able to be straight due to twisting and body alignment. The key is to stay as relatively straight as possible and to feel the same kind of even weight distribution and relaxation as in the standing position. The majority of the time the spine will stay straight length wise. Twisting often occurs as does the lower back curve, but the posture still remains straight and upright. The spine should never be arched or slouching over. This occurs by trying to over reach your limits within a movement. Initial discomfort and difficulties can happen due to weak back muscles, which commonly occur from lack of use and bad posture.

Building awareness of the posture and spine serves several purposes in tai chi practice. Tai chi contains many complex movements in which the body posture is not capable of being straight. By becoming aware of body posture and correct spinal alignment while standing, an understanding of what proper alignment feels correct. Proper alignment in the spine, along with the lower body, allows the body to become more stable and stronger while also exerting less energy. When the whole skeletal system starts to come into its own natural proper alignment, the body and its movements become more efficient.

Relaxation

After building a good posture in the spine, skeletal system, and lower body, awareness can then be brought to the muscles and connective tissues that hold it all together. Learning to relax the entire body is an important and prominent aspect of all tai chi practice. Muscles, lungs, tendons, ligaments, and joints should remain in a relatively relaxed state and never stretched or pushed to an extreme. The goal is to only put enough stress on the body to stimulate growth in flexibility and strength without putting any extreme pressure on the body. Deep relaxation affects the muscles, connective tissues, and eventually the whole body. The physical relaxation stimulated from proper body alignment can also be aided through mental focus allowing for deeper internal awareness.

As the body alignment in the lower body and spine are improved, the bones, tendons, ligaments, and other internal elements experience less stress. When the lower body is able to distribute the weight to the ground through a stable bone structure, the rest of the muscles need to do less work. This also occurs when the upper body is properly aligned and connected firmly to the base. The lower amount of stress and workload put on the body allows for the different tissues to relax more. With the improved relaxation in all the connective tissues it also becomes easier for the body to find and achieve these relaxed states due to increased flexibility.

As the entire body is put into proper alignment the rest of the body is able to relax, which in turn makes it easier to move in a relaxed state. As relaxation increases, movement will also use less energy or effort because of increased efficiency. The exact proper alignment at any given point in a movement is different depending on the individual. Through building a strong foundation in general body alignment and stability, awareness of proper alignment is developed. Through this awareness the individual will be able to feel when the body is relaxed or under unneeded pressure during the movement. Being able to feel the muscles, breathing, joints, etc. allows for control and the ability to consciously relax them. As the body relaxes it causes less stress and tension on the mind, which free the mind to also become more relaxed.

Bone Stacking Exercise

Begin by standing with the feet about shoulder width apart with the arms relaxed at the side. Gently and slowly shift the weight of the body from side to side. Keep both feet firmly on the ground and shift the majority of the weight onto one leg then without lifting up shift the weight to the other. As the body shifts from side to side a feeling of sinking lower into to the ground should begin.

What happens during this exercise can be thought of in the sense of a foundation of a building settling. When initially standing it feels as if the body (joints, tendons muscles, bones) are in a relaxed position, but as the weight is gently shifted from side to side the bones settles and the joints begin to fall into alignment. Sometimes this process is referred to as bone stacking because the bones are being stacked firmly together to form a solid base. Once the body (in this case primarily the lower part, legs and pelvis) "settles" then all the muscles and connective tissues can truly begin to relax because they are no longer being strained from improper alignment.

The mind is able to relax and focus on internal awareness to help aid in further developing complete body relaxation. Once the mind begins to become aware of each individual muscle they can all be focused on using the mind to become more relaxed and release tension. As the body starts to become more relaxed in all states including movement, the body will start to show and exhibit certain qualities. The muscles, joints, and connective tissues should remain relaxed through the full range of motions being practiced. Knowing that the body should attain these qualities also helps the mind to be aware of these specific qualities and also consciously try to exhibit them.

The result of this relaxation is part of the reason why many movements and postures are circular while keeping the body rounded. The body is rounded as the chest is being kept hollow with the arms extended in a relaxed manner. The hollow chest is created as a result of not stretching and rolling the shoulders all the way back, which opens the chest, rather the chest cavity is relaxed downward helping to sink and stabilize the center of gravity. The mind can become aware of the position of the limbs and correct them. The arms are extended yet relaxed enough for all the joints (shoulder, elbow and wrist) to remain unlocked, allowing for blood to flow more freely. Not all movements may exhibit such a circular shape, but all will contain an element of relaxation.

Water Relaxation Exercise

Begin by finding a comfortable sitting or standing position keeping the back straight. Allow the eyes to relax downward and focus on breathing slowly and deeply through the nose. Imagine a smooth flow of water flowing down on you, feeling the water flow over the entire body. As the water flows over the body feel each muscle relax and release the tension downward into the ground.

While imagining the water run over and through each part of your body. With each flow of water, relax each muscle as water passes through it. Any time or place that you feel resistance or tension focus on releasing it and allowing the water to wash it away. Continue to do this deeper and deeper into the body and eventually the mind. Over time and practice the relaxation will penetrate the entire body.

The initial stages of relaxing the body help the mind more easily find its own state of relaxation, in turn as the mind becomes more relaxed it is able to be more aware of the tensions within the body. The mental awareness can help to further relax the body deeper and more subtly. The body and mind help one another in achieving greater and more complete levels of relaxation.

While strengthening the body through proper alignment and positioning allows for greater relaxation in the body, the mind can have an equally strong affect. Feeling the relaxation in these muscles also increases the awareness of them. While initially the mind may focus on one aspect of development, such as relaxing a specific muscle, on breathing, or to quiet the mind, ultimately no direct thinking, focus, or intent will be needed, nor will any single aspect be the only aspect being developed. Instead the nature of these elements will be felt and understood subconsciously. The body and mind develop together and aid one another to reach a greater overall balanced level of relaxation.

A relative degree of relaxation is commonly practiced throughout all styles of tai chi. There are a number of reasons for these stemming from traditional thought and Daoist concepts. Some involve overcoming hardness with softness such as yin overcoming yang. Relaxation is also believed to be a key factor in many of the health benefits as mentioned in the chapters about tai chi characteristics. Oxygen and blood are able to move more smoothly and evenly through the tissues and organs when relaxed, as opposed to when tense. Once the body externally becomes relaxed, then tension internally can begin to be understood at a deeper level.

Different styles of tai chi build body awareness in a variety of ways, starting points, and progressions, yet all of them develop full body awareness through utilizing stability in structure, proper alignment, relaxation and mental focus. Some styles may focus more on building a strong base first and foremost, while another may be very particular about exact posture, yet eventually they lead to complete development and understanding of both. Wudang tai chi, still being practiced in Daoist temples, focuses a lot on relaxation as a part of preparation and practice for meditation and spiritual practices. Remember that just because one of these aspects of body awareness may be emphasized, that does not mean that the others are not also developed through

Empty stance 虚步

Common movement: White crane spreads its wings, Playing the lute

The empty stance is named so because the lead leg is only lightly touching the ground and not actually distributing much if any weight, thus leaving it empty. This stance is sometimes also named cat, false, or tricky stance.

While keeping the back straight, lower the body weight onto one leg, for maximum strength building try to squat until the thigh of the weight bearing leg is parallel to the ground (note that going that low can be very difficult and is advanced). The other leg extends forward while lightly touching the ground. The hips and feet both remain facing forward.

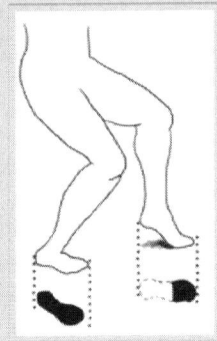

Empty Stance

Problems can involve where and how much weight to put on each leg, especially the front one. This stance helps with strengthening the legs and overall balance, because of all the weight being placed on a single leg.

practice. As the awareness of the body greatens, the overall strength becomes more noticeable and efficient. Eventually the awareness of one's own weight and center should also carry over into everyday life. Even when walking normally or performing everyday actions, a stable and firm rooting will occur even without making wide and low stances.

How aware of your body are you?

The body stays relaxed from the external muscles to ligaments and joints.

The body posture and alignment are key in tai chi. The spine should remain relatively straight.

The center of gravity should remain low in the body and distributed between the legs, which creates a strong foundation.

The feet should be firmly connected to the ground. The bottom of the feet should evenly contact the ground and creating a stable area for the body weight.

All these practices help the body in numerous ways. The rounded movements help with relaxation of joint and tendons relieving unneeded stress on the body. Correct spinal alignment has benefits to spine, and posture, training in stability increases leg strength and balance. Internal relaxation is the next step of body relaxation going deeper, often beginning by focusing on the breath.

Chapter 4
Breath Awareness

Anatomy * Awareness * Integration

> ### How aware of your breath are you?
>
> *Is the breath going in and out through the nose or mouth?*
>
> *When inhaling does the chest expand? the abdomen? both?*
>
> *Is breathing mostly being held in the chest? abdomen? throat? all?*
>
> *Which is longer inhalation or exhalation? or are they about equal?*
>
> *Is the breath deep or shallow? fast or slow?*

Breathing is one of the most important and significant actions that we do in order to live on a constant basis. With each breath we fuel the life in our bodies, oxygen comes in and carbon dioxide goes out. Every moment of our life is spent breathing. Breath is regulated and intertwined with nearly all core physiological systems including the musculoskeletal, nervous, cardiovascular, and endocrine systems. Without breath after only a few minutes we cease to live. Knowing that the breath is so important, it is important to be fully aware of it and understand it. How aware of your breath are you?

As body awareness develops and turns inward one of the first places to start is breathing. The lungs are one of the internal organs that we are already most aware of and can voluntarily control. Awareness of breath needs to be built up through first understanding the anatomy of breathing, then learning healthier and specific breathing techniques, while leading to regulating breath and connecting it to movement.

Anatomy

The process of breathing involves several parts of the body and is needed for functioning. Learning and knowing the different ways to use different parts of the anatomy involved in breathing and the function of helping the body in extracting oxygen from the air allows for more efficient breathing for whatever is being done. Following the path of the breath beginning with inhalation; there are two main ways to breathe in; through the nose or the mouth. From there the air flows to the lungs which can be utilized in a wide variety of techniques. These different methods of breathing use and affect a variety of internal organs and systems.

Air initially enters the respiratory system either through the mouth or the nose. When inhaling through the nostrils, the intake of air is limited to the speed and volume, but is subjected to being filtered before entering the lungs. When breathing through the mouth the air is not put through this extra filtering system, but larger volumes of air can be taken in more rapidly. Using the mouth for breathing also causes the loss of water and moisture through exposure. The nose is able to retain more of this water because less of the breath and surface area is directly exposed.

The nasal and mouth anatomy shows the main paths that air enters the body

Tai chi most often uses the nose for both inhalation and

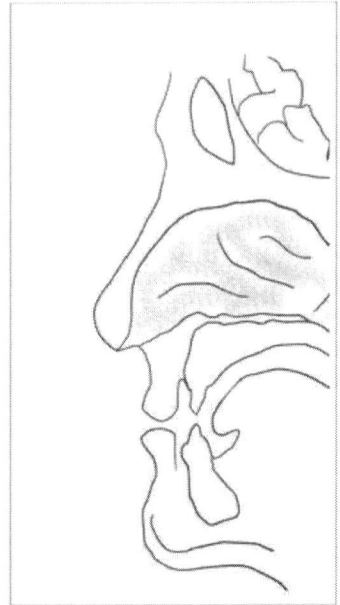

60

exhalation because of the advantages of extra filtering and better control at keeping the breath slow and smooth. Sometimes the mouth can be used for exhalation only. The advantages of using the mouth are not needed in tai chi since the movements do not require heavy breathing or a rapid exchange of oxygen. The emphasis is on long, full, deep breaths through the utilization of a greater lung capacity, rather than a rapid exchange of oxygen. Deeper breaths using more of the lungs will increase the amount of oxygen with each breath, which is important for metabolism in all bodily functions. Tai chi focuses on keeping a balance between inhalation and exhalation through the nose.

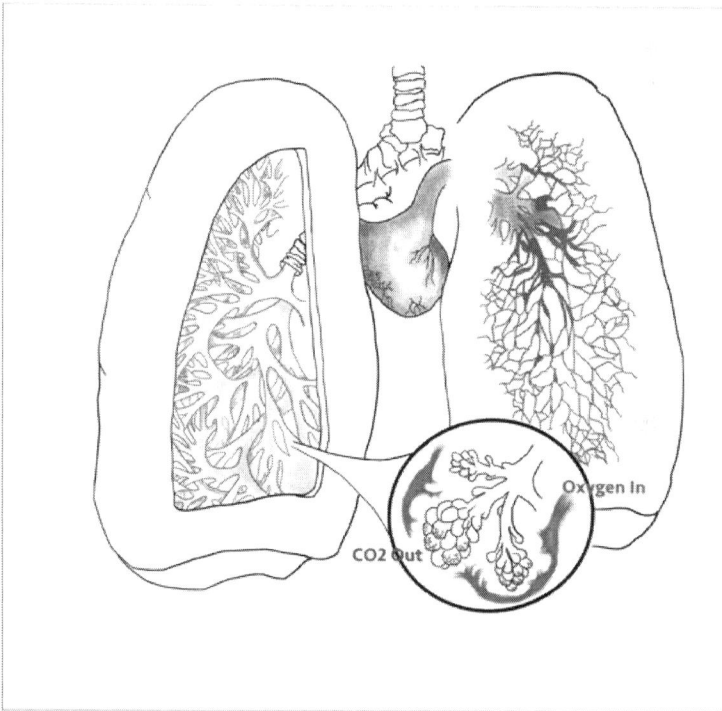

Air sac detail of CO2 and oxygen transfer.

The next step in the process that is greatly important in tai chi is the lungs. The primary purpose of the lungs is to deliver oxygen into and carbon dioxide out of the blood. Lungs harvest this oxygen to be used in fueling metabolism of molecules, like glucose, and release carbon dioxide. The lungs are comprised of long elastic bands or fibers of cartilage like tissue, which allows the lungs to expand and contract as we breathe. The inside of the lungs are covered with little air sacs that the lungs use to absorb oxygen from the inhaled air and transports it to the heart to be put into the blood stream.

While this is happening the blood is also transferring carbon dioxide out of the blood and into the air sacs. The air sacs then release the CO2 into the lungs which then expel the air during exhalation. The lungs can be filled partially or fully filled.

As the lungs expand the body has a number of ways of making room to allow for their expansion. The action of breathing can be caused and controlled by a number of muscles and methods, but the main group of muscles used is the thoracic diaphragm, often simply referred to as the diaphragm. Although it is not the only muscle involved, the movement of the diaphragm accounts for the majority of restriction and space affecting the lungs. It sits between the lungs in the upper chest cavity and the lower sac of organs in the abdomen, located just above the liver and the spleen.

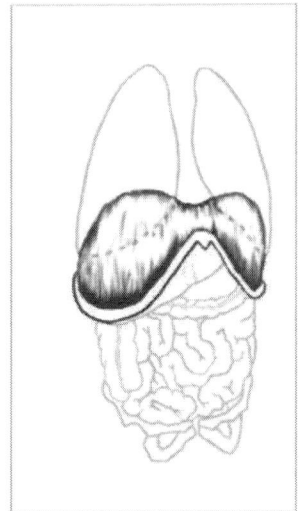

The diaphragm sits below the lungs and above the abdomen

This is a group of muscles that sits above stomach and liver, in a dome shape. When it relaxes it pushes down, opening the ribcage, decreasing pressure in the lungs, allowing air to enter the bottom of the lungs. Almost all breathing is a direct result of the action of the diaphragm. Relaxing the diaphragm creates low pressure within the chest cavity which causes air from outside the body, which is at a higher pressure, to fill the lungs. Depending on how much the diaphragm is allowed to relax can greatly affect how much the lungs get filled.

The process of breathing involves many more parts and can be affected by many other muscles as well. While the relaxation of the diaphragm allows for the most space and most direct way to give the lungs room for expanding, room can be made in other areas, such as within the ribcage, by using specific breathing techniques. During the beginning stages of breathing, learning to relax the diaphragm greater and filling the lungs greater are the most important parts to focus on improving. This relaxation allows for a fuller breath by the less restricted lungs which evidence has shown may lead to a longer life.

From knowing more about the anatomy, awareness of each of the organs individually, in groups, and as a whole can become greater. Development of the awareness of the anatomy and strengthening is often developed through using specific breathing techniques.

Breathing Techniques

Knowing the basic anatomy and physiology of breathing is the first step to building awareness. Feeling the full breath while controlling and relaxing the diaphragm for expanding the lungs is important. Awareness grows when slowing down the breath and focusing on each moment of it. There are many different breathing techniques used in practices throughout the world in a variety of disciplines such as sports, martial arts, meditation, singing, and weight lifting. The key breathing techniques used in the initial stages of tai chi practice are abdominal and reverse abdominal breathing, both maintain similar qualities.

Abdominal Breathing

In tai chi, as well as many other practices, breathing focused on the abdomen is most important. The type of breathing focused and used, especially in the initial stages of tai chi, is a type called abdominal breathing. This technique is referred to this way because the abdomen is used in controlling how and where the diaphragm and lungs are able to expand. Abdominal breathing can refer to any technique that involves expanding and contracting the abdomen in conjunction with breathing.

Abdominal breathing is often used interchangeably or in place of "natural" breathing. Natural breathing, sometimes called "Buddhist" breathing, focuses on expanding the abdomen during inhalation.

Natural breathing is when during inhalation the breath starts and feels as if it begins

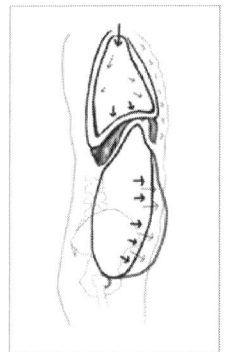

Abdominal Breathing

in the lower abdomen as it expands and fills up. Once the inhalation is complete, then smoothly begin to exhale. Do not hold the breath, make the transition from inhalation to exhalation seamless. During the exhale the abdomen should naturally, not forcefully, contract. Focus on developing the qualities of deeper, slower, smoother, relaxed, and balanced breathing.

This can be practiced by thinking and consciously expanding the lower abdomen during the initial stages of practice. The lungs should not be filled more than about 70% of max, this should be a feeling of being slightly full, but not any pressure in the chest or air held in the upper throat. Breathing through the abdomen allows for more relaxation because it takes pressure out of the ribcage. If the abdomen does not relax during inhalation the lungs may expand causing excess pressure within the ribcage, which is relatively confined, putting excess pressure on the vital organs within the chest cavity. The breath should be completely contained within the abdomen. When contained in only the abdomen it allows the lungs to expand fully, but not so much that strain is being put on other internal organs.

If it is difficult at first to feel or isolate the breath to the abdomen, while either sitting or standing with a straight back, begin by placing your right hand on the abdomen and the left hand on the chest. During inhalation the right hand should be being pushed out or raising as the abdomen expands, the left hand should feel no movement at all. If the left hand is moving, then the breath is not being isolated to the lower abdomen and unneeded pressure within all the organs in the chest is happening.

In general the benefits of abdominal breathing come from the action of contracting and relaxing the diaphragm. Efficiency in gas exchange and overall lung capacity decreases with age. By using abdominal the lungs expand fully to the bottom causing an overall increase in lung capacity. The abdomen is not surrounded by bones and thus allowed to expand without creating too much pressure on any of the organs. This slight pressure helps the intestines, liver, pancreas, etc. by stimulating and massaging them. This gentle massaging and stimulation increases circulation and sensitivity in all these organs. These benefits are seen in natural breathing as well as reverse abdominal breathing techniques. The different types of breathing serve different purposes. It is often easiest to start with normal abdominal, or natural, breathing.

70 % rule: Remember this rule when breathing. The lungs should never be filled to a forceful amount.

Reverse Abdominal Breathing

Reverse abdominal breathing is another type of abdominal breathing practiced in tai chi or in complementary exercises (e.g. meditation, qigong,.) This technique can be more difficult and is best learned under the guidance of a qualified teacher to ensure proper practice. This technique reverses the abdominal movements of normal breathing with respect to inhalation and exhalation. Reverse abdominal breathing is the way we used to breath as children. During inhalation the stomach contracts, while during exhalation the abdomen relaxes and expands slightly. This type of breathing is sometimes called "Daoist" breathing.

When first learning breathing awareness, this technique can often be more difficult to get used to and may take some conscious awareness to continuously breath in this fashion. Emphasis on reverse breathing often happens later as the body and breath awareness have been developed.

Reverse breathing is used to allow the energy to flow out and expand. The body relaxes allowing the oxygen rich blood to flow throughout the body. Reverse abdominal breathing has many of the same health benefits as normal abdominal breathing because the diaphragm is being worked in a similar way. The key differences lie in the expansion of the stomach to help increase the space for lungs to fill. While some of these lack, reverse abdominal creates even more internal massaging and benefits. This technique can be used to greater develop awareness and internal control.

Reverse breathing is important and used specifically for certain practices once one reaches an intermediate stage of their practice. Eventually this type of breath can be used when practicing the tai chi 28 form, but initially the practitioner should simply focus on any form of abdominal, normal abdominal breathing is often the easiest and most natural. More detail and advanced discussion about some of the more subtle changes that reverse abdominal breathing does will be discussed in greater detail in Book 2: Intermediate tai chi.

When practicing either technique during tai chi practice the breath will maintain common qualities. Some qualities are in the methods practiced and others are a result of the techniques practiced. The breath should become slower and longer. Tai chi refrains from using any kind of breath retention. During practice the breath should become seamless and even without any varying in speed during or between inhale and exhale. The transition between both the inhale and exhale should also become seamless, as one ends the next state should begin right after without any pause. Both the inhale and exhale will be of equal lengths and never pause or held in between.

When these kinds of breathing techniques are utilized regularly over time they will create an increase in lung capacity, which is a key part in building health and longevity. Lung capacity has shown a direct correlation as a predictor in overall mortality, especially those related to cardio vascular diseases. As we age the residual air left in the lungs after normal exhalation increases, and this left over CO_2 gets stuck in the air sacs, which is a primary symptom of chronic obstructive pulmonary disease.

By strengthening and conditioning the lungs through practice, the body benefits in other organs and systems. All of which increase overall health and longevity.

Throughout the practices and exercises in this book normal abdominal breathing will be used. Normal abdominal breathing is used at the beginning of practice because of the relaxing nature and fluid connection it builds between body and breath. This connection is often a key difficulty in the beginning of learning tai chi. Abdominal breathing helps to positively affect the body and help in progressing tai chi practice. Natural breathing benefits other organs through the diaphragm expanding into the abdominal cavity rather than putting pressure into the ribcage. By doing this the organs are lightly massaged and the lungs increase capacity while expanding to a greater degree.

Awareness of the breath and breathing techniques to help promote overall health is a key reason why tai chi emphasizes breath control. Once the breath can be felt, regulated, and solely focused on, then it can start to be felt throughout the body and working in coordination with all other parts.

Body and Breath

We are constantly moving creatures, throughout our daily life we move about from one place to another, doing one task or another. The breath unifies and gives life to the body allowing movement to take place. Breath is regulated and intertwined with nearly all core physiological systems including the musculoskeletal, nervous, cardiovascular, and endocrine systems. Becoming aware of the interconnectivity between breath and body is an important element in tai chi practice and everyday life. Learning how to coordinate the breath with movement allows the body to relax more while working more efficiently. The breath is inseparable from the body through the muscles directly involved in the breathing process, while tai chi further connects them by coordinating the breath with the movements of the rest of the body, and using breath control to regulate the speed of these movements.

Breathing directly affects muscles and organs throughout the body and not just the clear and obvious lungs. The movement of the lungs and diaphragm are also linked to other muscles in the body. One such muscle is the psoas The diaphragm is connected directly to the psoas, which in turn is connected to the hips and lower spine. Proper breathing and use of the diaphragm helps in aiding the relaxation of the psoas which can also help in achieving better posture and spinal alignment. Utilizing the abdominal muscles during the different breathing techniques helps to tone and condition the core muscles.

To begin building this awareness between breath and movement, focus on the breath while adding simple movements. An example of this can be found in the foundation exercises, specifically Foundation Exercise #1.

In tai chi practice each breath from the abdomen is coordinated with each movement. In general exhaling is done when the body is expanding or moving forward or at a time when one would exert any kind of energy or force. Inhaling is normally done when the body is receding, contracting, or relaxing.

After practicing proper abdominal breathing, the body should naturally begin to relax. When the breath has become deep, long, and even, the circulation will also begin to slow down, relieving stress internally. The muscles will naturally relax more and more with each exhale, in the same sense of relaxation and relief from sighing. Deep breathing will also help to relax deeper into the body with the diaphragm and internal organs.

Exercise

To begin feeling the link between movement and breath start by raising and lowering the arms with each inhalation and exhalation. Focus on slowing down and smoothing out the breath, as well as the arm movements.

Begin by standing with feet hip width apart, spine and neck straight with both hands resting in front of the body just below the navel. While inhaling raise the hands to shoulder level and while exhaling allow the hands to slowly fall down along the body to completely relax. Allow the muscles to relax downward slowly with the breath.

Coordinate the hands with the breath so that when half way through the inhale the hands should be half way to shoulder height. Continue to do this practice for a couple of minutes, while slowing down and deepening each breath. As the breath becomes deeper allow it to also become more relaxed and gentle. Imagine the air flowing in and out like a soft thread. Then let this relaxation to move beyond just the breath and into your movements. Allow the arms to weightlessly float up and sink down while staying totally relaxed.

As the movement gets coordinated with the breath, the body

becomes more efficient. Right after inhaling, the blood is oxygen rich, providing energy to be used and accessed quickly by body cells that need it. Expanding, moving forward, or striking all require more direct focused energy and are done while exhaling. In the opposite, when relaxing, retreating, or absorbing, the body needs to be relaxed which happens naturally when exhaling.

The timing of the breath with each movement should become more precise with regular practice. The relaxation in the body inward allows for the mind to also relax. Eventually the same level of relaxation and focus in breath control achieved in still seated or standing meditations can also be achieved while moving.

As the breath becomes deeper the movements should also begin to slow down. the slowing down of the movements help in

How aware of your breath are you?

Tai chi uses breathing through the nose into the lungs while allowing the abdomen to expand.

In normal practice the breath is mostly contained to the abdomen. During breathing only the abdomen should expand for the lungs, leaving the ribcage under little or no pressure.

In tai chi the breath almost always begins with expanding the lower lungs deep into the abdomen. If a deep breath is needed and expanding the abdomen is not enough then the breath continues to expand upward into the lungs and throat.

The breath should be deep, slow, and smooth; balanced with equal inhalation and exhalation.

awareness and developing efficiency. The type of breath that is used in still meditation, standing or sitting, is smooth slow and even, eventually this type of breath should be carried over into when movements are being done in tai chi. Since the movements are timed to go along with the breath, the movements should become slow and even and smooth the same as the breath.

Getting in touch with breath alone or with movement still carries all the benefits. Tai chi focuses on using abdominal breathing to increase longevity. This allows for greater relaxation and stimulating all parts of the body, such as the diaphragm, psoas, ribs, and chest.

Overall the breath is an important part of focus in tai chi. Learning to become aware of the minute details of the breath, its interaction with the body, along with its role in function and movement are key foundations on which the practice is built. Knowing and understanding the key anatomy of breathing helps to build this awareness. Using the nose during inhalation and exhalation helps to control the smooth steady flow of air and providing extra filtration. This cleaner more filtered air is used by the lungs to oxygenate the blood and keep the body functioning. Using specific breathing techniques utilizing the diaphragm, the breath becomes deep and full. These techniques, the most common and important being abdominal breathing, develop the qualities of slowness and smoothness without any form of retention becoming seamless between inhale and exhale. The breath also becomes directly linked to the body through all the muscles connected to them. The qualities of breath also influence and connect into the movements of the body. The breath along with the body awareness are the first stepping stones.

Chapter 5
Foundation Exercises

     Although tai chi is practiced in long sets of individual and unique movements linked together, there are also foundation exercises that benefit overall practice. These exercises help to unify breathing with movements of each part of the body. This coordination also develops slower and more relaxed movement throughout the body.

Upper Body

The first exercise is used to start coordinating the arm, shoulder, and hip movements with the breath. First practice the physical movements to gain muscle memory, and then focus more on the breath. The hands lift up and push out in coordination with the breath.

Purpose: Get in tune with expanding and contracting with inhalation and exhalation. Coordinate hand movements with breath. Lengthen the breath and slow down the movements.

Video supplements of each exercise can be found on YouTube by searching for the name of each move and Wudang tai chi or under the user Wudang Yogi.

Links to these YouTube videos can also be found at wesleychaplin.com/videos

Inhale: Begin by standing straight with the feet together, then begin to inhale and bend the knees shifting the weight onto the right leg (Image: 1.1.).

| 1.1 | 1.2 | 1.3 |

Exhale: The left begins to step to the left until the feet are shoulder width apart (Image: 1.2), as the exhale is completed the body weight should be evenly distributed between the legs and then sink down. (Image: 1.3).

Inhale:
Bring the hands slowly up to shoulder level (Images: 1.4-1.5). Near the end of the inhalation slightly draw the hands towards the chest (Image 1.6).

| 1.4 | 1.5 | 1.6 |

1.7

1.8

Exhale:
Push the hands straight
forward (Images 1.7-1.8).

Inhale:
Draw the hands back
towards the chest (Image
1.9).

1.9

1.10

1.11

1.12

Exhale:
Relax hands slowly down
(Images 1.10-1.12).

Continue to repeat and practice this movement for several
minutes while focusing on breathing with the abdomen. Allow the
arms to relax and flow as if rolling like the ocean tides,
seamlessly.

Lower Body

This exercise involves only using the legs and walking forward, practicing towards gaining the same kind of breath and body coordination as in the first exercise, except this exercise focuses on the legs rather than the arms. This exercise not only brings awareness between the movements of the legs with the breath, but it also gets used to the body weight moving in conjunction with the breath.

Begin by standing with the feet together in a relaxed position with knees slightly bent. The arms and hands should be relaxed at the sides, which remain at the sides throughout this entire exercise.

2.1

2.2

2.3

Inhale:

Sink the weight down and step the left foot forward at a 45 degree angle, keeping the majority of the weight on the right leg. (Images: 2.1-2.3)

Exhale:

Shift weight forward until centered and rooted, in a Bow stance (Images: 2.4-2.5)The timing of most exhales is coordinated with a forward movement

2.4

2.5

2.6

2.7

Inhale:

Shift the weight back onto the right leg by tucking the hip and sinking back. *Note: be careful not to lean back or raise up the center of gravity. (Images: 2.6-2.7)

2.8

2.9

Exhale: Shift the weight forward and bringing right foot together with the left foot. (Images: 2.8-2.9)

This exercise is then repeated on the right side.

2.10

Inhale:
Sink the weight down and step the right foot forward at a 45 degree angle, keeping the majority of the weight on the left leg. (Images: 2.10)

2.11

2.12

Exhale:
Shift the weight forward until centered and rooted in a right side Bow stance (Images: 2.11-2.12).

2.13

Inhale:
Shift the weight back onto the left leg by tucking the hip and sinking back. (Images: 2.13)

Note remember to be aware of the spine, is it straight and vertical? Make sure you are not bending/curving the spine or leaning backward.

Exhale:
Shift the weight forward and bring the left foot together with the right foot. (Images: 2.14)

2.14

At the end of doing this exercise once on each side it can then continue to be repeated from the start, e.g. after finishing the right side then repeat the left side. Continue practicing this exercise for several minutes by repeating it in a straight line if possible. Once the leg movements become natural and have been committed to muscle memory, remember to stay focused on deepening and slowing the breath while also slowing down and smoothing out the shifting of weight onto the legs. Other important things to watch and be aware of are rooting and stability feeling the weight shifts.

Combined Body

After having a grasp of coordinating and feeling the breath with the upper and lower body independently, next is to continue and coordinate both parts with the breath simultaneously. The next exercise combines the first two exercises, the upper body and the lower body exercises, of this section together. While walking also move the arms, both in coordination with the breath and each other.

Begin standing feet together, hands relaxed and comfortable at the side (Image 3.1).

3.1

3.2

3.3

Inhale:
Slightly sink the weight to the right leg and begin moving the left foot forward 45 degrees to step, while lifting both hands up staying close to the front of the torso (Image 3.2). As the inhale completes, the left leg should be firmly rooted but still not holding much of the weight, while the hands reach up to about chest or shoulder level (Image 3.3).

Exhale:
Shift the weight forward more onto the left leg, coming into a Bow stance, while pushing forward with the hands away from the chest. The resulting position is in a Bow stance with both hands extended forward at chest or shoulder level. (Images: 3.4)

3.4

3.5

3.6

Inhale:
Shift the majority of the weight back onto the right leg into something similar to Empty stance, while the hands draw back towards the chest (Images 3.5-3.6).

3.7

3.8

Exhale:
Step forward bringing the right foot together with the left foot, while the hands relax down at the sides (Images 3.7-3.8).

This is the complete movement for the left side.

When doing this exercise try to focus on the same things that were focused on when doing each of the movements separately. This exercise is the beginning of getting the entire body to relax in movement with the breath.

This movement can also be repeated on the right side as well.

Inhale slightly sinking the weight to the left leg and begin moving the right foot forward to step, while lifting both hands up staying close to the front of the torso. (Image 3.9-3.11)

3.9

3.10

3.11

As the inhale completes, the right leg should be firmly rooted but still not holding much of the body weight, while the hands reach up to about chest or shoulder level.

Exhale:
Shift the weight forward more onto the right leg while pushing forward with the hands away from the chest. The resulting position is in a Bow stance with both hands extended forward at chest or shoulder level (Image 3.12).

3.12

Inhale:
Shifting the majority of the weight back onto the left leg, while the hands draw back towards the chest (Image 3.13-3.14).

3.13

3.14

3.15

Exhale:
Step forward bringing the left foot together with the right foot, while the hands relax down at the sides (Image 3.15).

At the end of doing this exercise once on each side it can then continue to be repeated from the start, e.g. after finishing the right side then repeat the left side. Continue practicing this exercise for several minutes by repeating it in a straight line if possible. Once the leg and arm movements become natural and have been committed to muscle memory, remember to stay focused on deepening and slowing the breath while also slowing down and smoothing out the body movements.

Torso

After starting to get into tune with coordinating upper and lower body movements with breath, it is important to continue by getting the body used to the circular movements found throughout tai chi. These movements take place not only in the limbs but also throughout the body in the form of spinning, twisting and rotating every part of the body including the spine, torso, and weight displacement.

Standing feet hip width apart with a straight back, bring both hands in front of the chest as if holding a ball (Images: 4.1-4.3).

4.1   4.2   4.3

Keeping the palms facing each other, rotate the imaginary ball so that the left hand is on top facing downward where the right palm should be on the bottom facing upward. (Images: 4.4-4.5)

4.4   4.5

During this exercise also practice shifting the weight from side to side as the ball is rotated, shift the weight in the direction of the hand on top. While shifting the weight allow the shoulders and hips to face the opposite direction of the top hand.

| 4.6 | 4.7 | 4.8 | 4.9 |

Then rotate the hands so that the left hand is on the bottom and the right hand is on the top (Images: 4.6-4.9). The path in which the hands move to reach these positions can vary. The easiest way to begin is to simply move the hands as if turning a steering wheel. Once more familiar and comfortable with turning the hands the other movement paths can and should be explored. This movement should not only be practiced in a flat circle but rather sphere. No matter what path the hands take though, the palms should always be facing each other.

| 4.10 | 4.11 | 4.12 | 4.13 |

Then repeat this exercise on the other side, rotating the hands so that the left hand is on the bottom and the right hand is on the top (Images: 4.10-4.13).

87

| 4.14 | 4.15 | 4.16 | 4.17 |

After feeling comfortable with this movement and it begin to become more fluid, the ball can be "rotated" in any directions. To build up this exercise it is first practiced rotating the ball using only the hands, but eventually using the whole body in the motion, specifically shoulders and hips (Images 4.14-4.21).

Much of the body movement comes from the strength of the waist and suppleness and twisting of the spine. This is a source for a lot of internal power and core training. The twisting and rotation also carries out into the limbs. As discussed before the limbs and torso in a relaxed position keep a rounded position, this is seen in the movements as well.

| 4.18 | 4.19 | 4.20 | 4.21 |

| 4.22 | 4.23 | 4.24 | 4.25 |

To finish the movement, normally a closing movement is done at a point when the body is facing forward with the hips and shoulders facing squarely forward. As the hands reach a position in which they are facing each other and placed on each side of the body, take a deep breath in allowing the hands to face the ground (Image 4.26). Exhale and relax as the hands slowly fall towards the ground and eventually to the sides of the body, once the body is relaxed return the left foot to the right foot (Image 4.27-4.29).

| 4.26 | 4.27 | 4.28 | 4.29 |

Part 3

Wudang Form

Chapter 6

Wudang Tai Chi 28 Short Form

起势 Opening Sequence

Chinese name: **起势**
Pinyin: qǐ shì
Translation: Opening sequence
Other names:

The beginning of the form prepares the body by coordinating the breath with movement, establishing a firm stance, and calming the mind. Focus on the breath during these first initial movements and allow the muscles to relax. The movements are kept simple and done while standing stationary allowing the breath and movements to slow and smoothen, helping set a baseline speed at which the rest of the form should be done.

Video supplements of each individual move and the form in its entirety can be found on you tube by searching for the name of each move and Wudang tai chi or under the user Wudang Yogi.

Links to these YouTube videos can also be found at wesleychaplin.com/videos

Begin by standing with the feet together in a relaxed position, with a straight spine, tucked pelvis, and a slight bend in the knees (Image 1.1).

Inhale: Sink the weight slightly, shifting to the right foot and begin raising the left foot (Image 1.2).

1.1

1.2

1.3

1.4

Exhale: Take the left foot and finish stepping directly to the left at about shoulder width apart. Upon finishing the exhale sink and root both the feet (Image 1.3-1.4).

Inhale: Raise the arms to the sides until about shoulder height (Image 1.5-1.6) and at the end of the breath draw them in towards the shoulders slightly (Image 1.7-1.8).

1.5

1.6

1.7

1.8

Exhale:
After drawing in slightly begin to push outward to the sides (Image 1.9-1.10).

1.9

1.10

1.11

1.12

Inhale:
Breath deep and long, raising the arms to the top of the head while filling the belly (Image 1.11-1.12).

Exhale:
Once the hands have reached the top of the head relax while exhaling and bring the hands down in front of the body (Image 1.13-1.16).

1.13

1.14

1.15

1.16

The arms will relax and fall to the sides and the body weight will sink with a slight bend in the knees (Image 1.17-1.18). At the end of this exhale the body should be relaxed and the movement coordinated with the breath. This opening sequence of movements is often used in several Wudang tai chi practices to begin practice.

1.17

1.18

After this point in the book the breathing will no longer be specified, not because it is not important, but rather for simplicity and to not overwhelm the beginner. At the beginning stages just learning the movements and body postures is most important.

Bring the fingertips together slightly while raising both arms in front of the body. The arms should also bend a little at the elbows (Image 1.19-1.20).

1.19

1.20

1.21   1.22   1.23   1.24

Arms:
With both hands still raised, move the right hand in a counter clockwise direction towards the center of the body circling back outward in front of the body to eventually stop at the top of the ball (Image 1.21-1.25).

1.25   1.26

Legs:
While the upper body is moving the weight should be shifted first onto the left leg as the right arm rotates out (Image 1.21-1.23), while returning to being centers as the arm completes the rotation (Image 1.24-1.26).

1.27

1.28

1.29

Arms:

After the right hand completes this movement, the left hand circles out (Image 1.26-1.30) and downward to form the bottom of the ball. (Image 1.31)

Legs:

The weight is then shifted onto the right leg the left as the hand begins to rotate out (Image 1.27-1.30), the left leg is then brought together with the right leg as the left hand completes its rotation (Image 1.31-1.33).

1.30

1.31

1.32

退步崩式 Step back and strike straight

Chinese name: 退步崩式
Pinyin: tuì bù bēng shì
Translation: step back and strike straight
Other names:

This is the first actual movement after the initial opening. The name and movement are pretty straight forward in describing the action and purpose, in which one first steps back before stepping forward advancing both the upper and lower body. The leading arm moves straight from the lower hip upward toward chest level, this movement is the straight strike part of the name.

2.1   2.2   2.3

Arms:
The left arm (while remaining curved slightly) rises from the bottom of the circle until it reaches about shoulder height. The right hand will continue to push forward just below the height of the left arm (Image 2.1-2.6).

Legs:
Stepping back at a 45 degree angle to the left with the left foot (Image 2.1-2.6).

Torso:
As the body rotates, shift forward.

2.4   2.5   2.6

This ends the straight blow to the left side and now it is done on the right side after a transition movement.

Transition

| 2.7 | 2.8 | 2.9 | 2.10 |

Arms:
Continue pushing the right hand forward while rotating the palm to face the body, while doing the opposite with the left hand, recede and turn the palm away from the body (Image 2.8-2.10). Then begin to recede rotating the hands while maintaining a ball shape and turn to the right (Image 2.11-2.14).

Legs:
The body weight at first will shift slightly forward onto the left leg (Image 2.8-2.9), then as the body rotates the weight is shifted between the legs (Image 2.10-2.13).

Torso:
The shoulder and chest follow the hip as the legs rotate to the right.

| 2.11 | 2.12 | 2.13 | 2.14 |

100

Arms:
Bring the right hand to the bottom and the left hand to the top to form a ball (Image 2.15-2.16).

2.15

2.16

Legs:
As the body finishes turning the right foot is brought back towards the left foot. (Image 2.14) Finish rotating and step back bringing the right foot together with the left foot.(Image 2.15-2.16).

That ends the transition movement and then the step back for forward blow is done on the right side.

Arms:
The right arm (while remaining curved slightly) rises from the bottom of the circle until it reaches about shoulder height. The left hand will continue to push forward just below the height of the left arm (Image 2.17-2.19).

Legs:
Stepping forward at a 45 degree angle to the right with the right foot (Image 2.17-2.19).

Torso:
As the body rotates and shifts forward (Image 2.17-2.19).

2.17

2.18

2.19

揽雀尾　Grasp the sparrow's tail

Chinese name: 揽雀尾
Pinyin: lǎn què wěi
Translation: Grasp the sparrow's tail
Other names:

Grasping the sparrow's tail is a common movement found throughout many different styles of tai chi. This movement helps get the body used to shifting the weight and rotating. The movement also contains several positions that utilize only one leg to distribute the weight, which help to increase overall balance and leg strength.

Relax both hands and face the palms downward while sinking the weight (Image 3.1-3.3).

   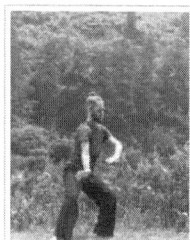

| 3.1 | 3.2 | 3.3 | 3.4 |

Arms: Sweep the arms across the front of the body (to the left) slightly arcing upward near the end of the movement (Image 3.4-3.9).

Legs: The legs shift out of a Bow stance facing the right to a Bow stance facing the left (Image 3.4-3.9). To do this, the left foot will turn left just before the body weight is shifted back onto the left leg and the right foot and leg turn left as well (Image 3.4-3.8). At the end the weight shifts forward onto the left leg into a Bow stance (Image 3.8).

Torso: During this movement the whole body should follow the motion of the hands by rotating to the left and shifting the weight in that direction (Image 3.4-3.8).

| 3.5 | 3.6 | 3.7 | 3.8 |

Repeat for the opposite side:

3.9   3.10   3.11

Arms:
Relax both hands and face the palms downward while sinking the weight (Image 3.9-3.11). Sweep the arms across the front of the body to the right (Image 3.9-3.11).

Legs:
The legs shift out of a Bow stance facing the left (Image 3.10) to a Bow stance facing the right (Image 3.11). To do this the right foot will turn just before the body weight is shifted back onto the right leg, while the left foot and leg turn to the right. At the end, the weight shifts forward onto the right leg into a Bow stance (Image 3.11).

Torso:
During this movement the whole body should follow the motion of the hands by rotating to the left and shifting the weight in that direction. Near the end of the movement start shifting the weight onto the back (left) leg while keeping the hips and body facing front (Image 3.11).

That ends the first part of the movement which is sweeping across the sides implementing the tai chi idea of press down.

3.12

3.13   3.14   3.15   3.16

Arms: Raise the left hand, keeping the right hand pointing fingers down. Bring the left hand and forearm downward across the right arm, while simultaneously raising the right arm (Image 3.12-3.16).

Legs: Step forward bringing left foot to right foot (Image 3.14-3.16).

Torso: The entire body will turn slightly left while stepping forward and sinking the weight (Image 3.14-3.16).

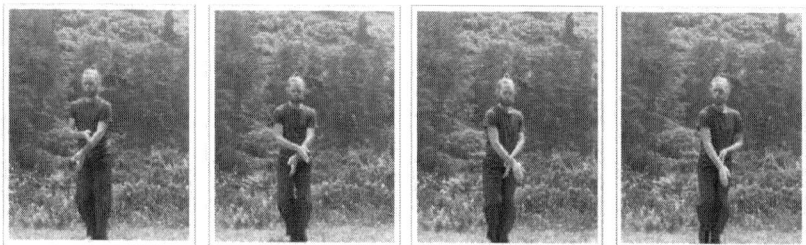

3.17   3.18   3.19   3.20

Arms: Raise the right arm up and over the left arm which is close to the body fingers pointing to the ground (Image 3.17-3.18). Bring the right hand and forearm downward across the left arm, while simultaneously raising the left arm (Image 3.19-3.20).

Legs: The weight gets shifted from the right leg all the way onto left leg as the body twists leftward (Image 3.17-3.20).

Torso: The body should slightly untwist and raise. While sinking the weight down twist left (Image 3.17-3.20).

Arms:
Cross the arms in front of the body keeping them horizontal and in front of the mid section (Image 3.21-3.22).

Legs:
Raise the right leg bent, foot covering knee of left leg which is slightly bent (Image 3.21-3.22).

Torso:
Remains facing forward.

3.21

3.22

Arms:
Keeping the palms facing out open the arm outward in front of the body (Image 3.23-3.25).

Legs:
Make a heel kick forward, straightening the right leg forward and keeping the foot flexed (Image 3.23-3.25).

3.23

3.24

3.25

| 3.26 | 3.27 | 3.28 |

Arms:
The arms circle outward down towards the hips before scooping up. With the right palm facing up moving slightly upward from a lower position, while the left palm facing down will be moving mostly forward from a higher position closer to shoulder level (Image 3.26-3.30).

Legs:
Bring the right leg back to a bent position (Image 3.26) before stepping forward with the right leg and shifting the weight in that direction (Image 3.27-3.30).

Torso:
Facing right and forward in line with the right foot.

| 3.29 | 3.30 |

Arms:
While sinking the weight rotate the hands to the left and slightly bring the elbows in (Image 3.31).

Legs:
Stay in the same position while sinking the weight and lowering the body (Image 3.31).

3.31

Arms:
While rotating keep the hands and arms in the same position in reference to the hips, around shoulder height (Image 3.32-3.34).

Legs:
Rotate towards the left. While rotating, shift the weight from the right leg to the left leg, while allowing the feet to also rotate so that they face the same direction as the hips (Image 3.32-3.34). Remember to rotate the feet keeping the heels on the ground.

Torso:
Twist and rotate both hips and shoulders to the left (Image 3.32-3.34).

3.32

3.33

3.34

108

| 3.35 | 3.36 | 3.37 |

Arms:
Rotate the arms and palms so that the right palm is now facing downward and the left facing upward (Image 3.35-3.37).

Legs:
Step forward bringing the right foot together with the left foot. Once the feet are together, continue to sink the weight and root slightly (Image 3.35-3.37).

| 3.38 | 3.39 | 3.40 | 3.41 |

Arms:
While rotating, slowly bring the arms across the front of the body while maintaining them at shoulder height (Image 3.38-3.41).
Legs:
Step back with the right foot at a 45 degree angle from the original center line (Image 3.38) and shift the weight towards the right leg while rotating the body in that direction (Image 3.39-3.41).

This is the end of the upper grab of the tails and leads to the forward finger strike.

Arms:

While shifting back, the right arm continues moving in the sweeping circle previously, it will continue in a circular path downward toward the right hip bone. In following this arc naturally the right palm should finish facing upward. The left will move a much shorter distance and should finish in front of the solar plexus about a foot away (Image 3.42-3.44).

3.42   3.43   3.44

Legs:

Sink the weight back onto the left leg keeping the hips facing forward. In doing this the front leg, right leg, should straighten (Image 3.42-3.44).

 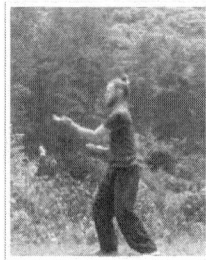

3.45   3.46

Arms:
While stepping forward bring the right hand forward and up at a 45 degree angle with the fingers extended up to just above eye level. As the right hand comes up the left hand will trace just along down the outside of the right arm. As if the left hand were pushing up the sleeve on the right arm up to the elbow (Image 3.45-3.49).

Legs:
Shift the weight forward and bring the feet together towards the right foot (Image 3.45-3.49).

3.47

3.48

3.49

3.50

3.51

Arms:
Right hand will circle towards the outside of right side and sweep towards the ground (Image 3.50-3.53).

Legs:
Sink the weight and lower towards the floor by bending the knees and squatting. Keep the back straight, to reach down it is better to bend at the waist and don't hunch the back. (Image 3.50-3.53).

Torso:
While remaining low to the ground twist the body and feet 45 degrees. Sweep the right hand and arm across the body to the left while rotating (Image 3.50-3.53).

3.52

3.53

3.54

| 3.55 | 3.56 | 3.57 | 3.58 |

Arms:
Keeping the upper arm close to the body while hinging at the elbow, the right hand raises with the forearm upward to the height of the head . The left hand remains on the outside of the right hand and arm near the elbow (Image 3.55-3.58).

Legs:
Stand up while keeping your center focused in the lower abdomen. Plant both feet together in the ground, you will now be facing 180 from start position (Image 3.55-3.58).

| 3.59 | 3.60 | 3.61 |

At the end of this movement rotate the right wrist and bring the fingers together- forming a crane like beak. The left hand will come to elbow height palm facing upward. (Image 3.59-3.61)

Section 4

正单鞭 Straight single whip

Chinese name: 正单鞭
Pinyin: zhèng dān biān
Translation: Straight single whip
Other names:

Single whip is a common move found in many different styles of tai chi. The name comes from the way the energy and force is transferred through the body out into the hand. Like cracking a whip, the force builds up and gathers force as it travels from the ground through the body, and focused out through the hand.

Starting from the end of Grasping the sparrows tail (Image 4.1), this move is performed in several ways throughout the tai chi 28 and 108 form. The key difference is that sometimes it is done with a kick, and other times the kick is omitted, going directly into the core movement. The first time single whip is done in the 28 form it is done with the kick, and is as follows:

4.1

114

Arms:
Remain stationary with left hand facing palm down just below the right elbow. The right arm should be bent with the hand clasped and the fingers pointed together (Image 4.3-4.6).

Legs:
Sink the weight down onto the right leg and root while raising the left leg bending at the knee with the left foot slightly flexed (Image 4.2). The left leg is then extended outward and up as high as flexibility allows (Image 4.3-4.4).

Torso:
The body will continue facing mostly forward and only turn slightly to the left as the leg kicks out (Image 4.3-4.4).

4.2   4.3   4.4

It is most important to keep the balance on one leg throughout this movement. For this reason it is important to bring the left leg back to the right leg before stepping forward (next move). Sometimes people will just fall forward and let their leg fall to the ground, rather than actually taking the step. Tai chi is about gaining awareness and control of the body, balance, and weight.

Arms:
The arms remain stationary
(Image 4.5-4.7).

Legs:
Bring the left leg back
bending at the knee and
then lower it next to the
right foot (Image 4.5-4.7).

4.5

4.6

Torso:
Stationary (Image 4.5-4.7).
It is at this point that the move can also be started from by
omitting the kick.

4.7

4.8

4.9

Arms:
The left hand will start to cross the chest and the right hand will
slightly relax, while the waist will begin to rotate to the left. The
left hand will sweep across the front of the body continuing to
extend forward (Image 4.7-4.12).

Legs:
Begin by stepping to the left, preparing for shifting into a Bow
stance. Continue with the left foot, shifting the weight forward to
a Bow stance (Image 4.7-4.12).

Torso:
While shifting forward remember to rotate the waist and hips so that they face left (Image 4.7-4.12).

4.10　　　　　　　4.11　　　　　　　4.12

The movement should coordinate to get the feeling of a whip like motion from the right foot transferring to the arm extending forward striking with the ridge of the hand.

That is the first single whip done in this form and is the main movement for which it is named; it is what is most commonly seen in all styles of tai chi. That is also where the movement normally ends (Image 4.12), however in 28 the first single whip continues by applying the same principles in a forward strike. The lower body, legs, waist etc are in a different position and thus the source of power and stability origins are different, but the methods of allowing the power to travel through the relaxed body and crack out like a whip are the same.

4.13　　　　　　　4.14　　　　　　　4.15

Arms:
The left arm circles out and towards the left hip (Image 4.13-4.15).

Legs:
The weight is shifted back onto the right leg as the left leg turns inward to the right ending in a Horse Stance (Image 4.13-4.16).

Torso:
The upper body rotates to the right along with the left leg (Image 4.13-4.16).

4.16

4.17

4.18

Arms:
The right arm stays elevated at shoulder height while the left arm pushes forward from the left hip up to about chest level (Image 4.16-4.18).

Legs:
The weight is shifted slightly to the right leg as it bends. The left leg straightens, creating a Bow stance with the feet pointing slightly forward- the feet should naturally rotate to the right (Image 4.16-4.18).

Torso:
The body remains facing mostly forward in the direction of the left hand. Both the left hip and shoulder will be further forward (Image 4.16-4.18).

提手上式 Raise the hands

Chinese name: 提手上式
Pinyin: tí shǒu shàng shì
Translation: Raise hand upward
Other names:

This movement is named for the seemingly simple movement that is balance, power, and martial application.

Video supplements of each individual move and the form in its entirety can be found on you tube by searching for the name of each move and Wudang tai chi or under the user Wudang Yogi.

Links to these YouTube videos can also be found at wesleychaplin.com/videos

| 5.1 | 5.2 | 5.3 |

Arms:

The right arm relaxes facing palm down at around waist height while the left arm moves slightly left and down towards the waist facing palm down (Image 5.1-5.3). Both arms move to the right with the body (Image 5.2-5.3).

Legs:
The legs only move slightly more to the right as more weight is placed on the right leg (Image 5.1-5.3).

  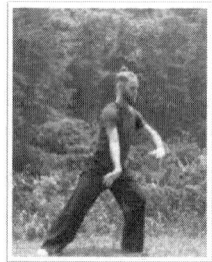

| 5.4 | 5.5 | 5.6 |

Arms:
Both arms relax downward to just below chest level, then they sweep across and with the body to the left (Image 5.4-5.9).

Legs:
The weight is shifted back onto the left leg after turning the foot outward. The right foot then turns with the body before being brought toward the left foot (Image 5.4-5.9).

Torso:
As the weight sinks and is shifted toward the left leg, the torso will also rotate slightly in that direction. (Image 5.4-5.6).

| 5.7 | 5.8 | 5.9 |

Arms:
As both hands circle around to the left hip (Image 5.7-5.11), the right hand will grip fingertips together and remain straightened when raised straight up (Image 5.13-6.5.15). Keeping straightened fingers the left hand faces the right wrist with palm open and follows the right wrist upward.

Legs:
The weight is shifted completely onto the left foot, rooting down with a slight bend in the leg. (Image 5.7-5.12.). The right leg rises with a bend at the knee, then extends forward kicking knee height (Image 5.13-5.15).

| 5.10 | 5.11 | 5.12 |

5.13 5.14 5.15

Arms:
While stepping forward lift the right hand upward at shoulder level extended three quarters of the way, with the elbow in line with the knee, the left arm will lower slightly but stay near same height shifting back and stay close to the front of the chest (Image 5.16-5.18).

Legs:
Bring the right leg back by bending it at the knee (Image 5.16), Step forward with the right leg in the direction you are facing, resulting in a Bow stance (Image 5.17-5.18).

Torso: As a result of this arm position, the shoulders and hips will be facing a 45 degree angle with the right side more forward. (Image 5.18).

5.16 5.17 5.18

5.19

5.20

5.21

Arms:

During this rotation the hands will stay in facing each other as they flip during the rotation. The right hand will turn from facing up to facing downward, while the left will go from facing downward to facing up, and both hands will stop near waist height (Image 5.19-5.24).

Legs:

Keeping the feet in the same relative position rotate them both to the left as much as possible. Initially more weight will be placed on the right leg , but as the rotation finishes the left leg will start bearing more weight (Image 5.19-5.24).

Torso:

The entire twists and rotates a full 180 to the left (Image 5.19-5.24).

5.22

5.23

5.24

123

白鹤亮翅 White crane spreads its wings

Chinese name: 白鹤亮翅
Pinyin:bái hè liàng chì
Translation: White crane spreads its wings
Other names: Crane spreads its wings

In Chinese culture and history the crane has been regarded as an animal representative of longevity, seen especially in Daoism, and has carried these ideas through to the names and characteristics of some tai chi movements. The final position of this movement with the arms extended and open resembles that of a crane spreading open its wings. This move is highly common in several types of tai chi, and represents the splitting of yin and yang.

Starting from the final position of Raise the hands (image 5.24)

6.1

6.2

6.3

Arms:
Both hands form a ball with the right hand on the bottom by circling to the right as the body turns (Image 6.1-6.6).

Legs:
Both feet turn to the left as the weight is shifted back off the left leg and evenly between the legs (Image 6.1-6.3). Take a small step forward with the right foot beginning to shift the weight forward onto it (Image 6.4-6.6).

Torso:
The body rotates to the right so that both the shoulders and hips are facing 90 degrees to the right from the starting position.

6.4

6.5

6.6

6.7

6.8

6.9

Arms:

Open the arms so that the left hand lowers down and out to about hip level, while the right hand opens up and out to about head level (Image 6.7-6.12).

Legs:

Shift the weight onto the right leg and move the body forward until the feet are together (Image 6.7-6.9). Extend the left foot forward slightly and lightly touching the ground, keep the majority of the weight on the right leg, finally lower the weight down into base of the right foot (Image 6.10-6.12).

Torso:

Stationary (Image 6.7-6.12).

6.10

6.11

6.12

左搂膝拗步　Left brush the knee and twist step

Chinese name: 左楼膝拗步
Pinyin: zuǒ lóu xī ǎo bù
Translation: Left brush knee twist step (stance)
Other names: Brush knee

Brush knee is practiced in almost all tai chi styles because it is a relatively simple movement while still containing many of the key elements of tai chi. The body rotates as the leading hand brushes down by the knee, while the opposite hand raises and pushes forward. This movement helps develop coordination between all parts of the body in rotating and moving forward while keeping balance between opposing forces. In Zhang Sanfeng tai chi 28 form this movement is only practiced on the left side, but in other forms (e.g. Tai chi 108 form) and exercises, Brush Knee is practiced alternating on both sides repeatedly.

Transitioning from the ending position of White Crane spreads its wings. (Image 7.1)

7.1

7.2

7.3

Arms:
The right arm will sweep across the chest (Images 7.3) before arcing down across the left side of the body (Images 7.4) to form the bottom part of the ball (Images 7.5). As the right hand begins to fall the left hand finishes its arc upward (Images 7.2-7.4) to form the top of the ball (Images 7.5).

Legs:
The weight of the body will shift slightly forward onto the left leg (Images 7.3) before it is all shifted back onto the right leg (Images 7.4). As the hands begin to form the ball, the left foot should step together with right leg (Images 7.5).

Torso:
The body will rotate with the formation of the ball to the right about 90 degrees (Images 7.2-7.6).

7.4

7.5

Arms:
The left hand sweeps across the chest and arcs down (Images 7.6), falling to the side, arcing forward and outward brushing past the left knee (Images 7.8-7.9). The right hand simultaneously comes to chest level and then pushes straight forward (Images 7.7-7.9)

7.6   7.7   7.8

Legs:
Standing with feet together, step forward to the left slightly with the left leg, while keeping the majority of the weight on the right leg (Images 7.7). Shift the weight forward onto the left leg coming into a Bow stance (Images 7.8-7.9).

Torso:
Rotate the upper body to face the direction you are stepping (Images 7.7). The body rotates to the left to square up the shoulders and hips in the direction the right hand is pushing (Images 7.7-7.9).

7.6 (side view)   7.7 (side view)   7.9

129

In the 28 form this movement is only practiced on the left side, although it is often practiced on both sides, left and then right. The movements are simply mirrored.

To practice brush knee on the right side begin with the ending of left brush knee.

Arms:
Hands rotate into a ball position with the right hand on top.

Legs:
Standing with feet together, step forward slightly to the right with the right leg while keeping the majority of the weight on the left leg.

Torso:
Rotate the upper body to face the direction you are stepping.

Then continue...

Arms:
The left hand falls to the side, arcing forward and outward brushing past the left knee. The right hand simultaneously comes to chest level and then pushes straight forward.

Legs:
Shift the weight forward onto the left leg coming into a Bow stance.

Torso:
The body moves rotates slightly to the left to square up in the direction forward.

手挥琵琶 Hands strumming the lute

Chinese name: 手挥琵琶
Pinyin: shǒu huī pí pá
Translation: Hands strum the lute
Other names: Old man plays the lute, playing the pipa

The final position of the hands in this movement resemble the position of the hands holding and playing a Chinese instrument known as a pipa. A pipa looks similar to a guitar that is played in an upright position and is often translated as a "lute."

This movement follows after a variety of different moves depending on the form and style of tai chi, in this case, the Wudang 28 form, the starting position follows the final movement of left brush knee.

131

8.1 8.2 8.3

Arms:
Both arms circle towards the sides of the body whilst falling towards the hips (Images 8.1-8.2).

Legs:
The right foot comes forward together with the left leg (Images 8.1-8.2).

Torso:
Keep the shoulders and hips stable and facing forward, while shifting straight forward without twisting (Images 8.1-8.2).

8.1 (side view) 8.2 (side view) 8.3 (side view)

Arms:
Allow the arms to arc out slightly while raising up to between chest and shoulder height (Images 8.3)

Legs:
The weight should finish shifting forward and then all the weight will be shifted onto the right leg. The left leg will lift, getting ready to go into Empty stance, Empty stance (Images 8.3).

Torso:
Naturally stationary.

The hands should be slightly staggered with the left hand in front, and both hands fingers pointing forward (Images 8.3).

Arms:
Both arms will relax downward bending at the elbows and wrists. The right arm should lower about a foot below the left arm (Images 8.4).

8.4

Legs:
The majority of the weight will remain on the right leg as the left leg steps slightly forward into Empty stance (Images 8.4).

Torso:
The body weight will sink down and the chest remain curved and hollow (Images 8.4).

8.4 (side view)

上步搬拦锤 Step forward, parry, and punch

Chinese name: 上步搬拦捶
Pinyin: shàng bù bān lán chuí
Translation: Step forward, move, block, punch
Other names:

The name describes each of the key martial aspects of this movement. The movements can be divided into two pairings: step forward and parry; block and punch. While stepping forward the body sinks and twists slightly downward and back to parry. As the weight and torso shifts forward the left arm stays raised and blocks while the right hand comes forward underneath it.

Step Forward and Parry

Although this movement follows many different movements throughout different forms, the transition into this movement is normally short.

9.1   9.2   9.3

Arms:
The right hand begins moving upward toward shoulder height while the left hand lowers sweeps down toward the left hip. (Image 9.1-9.3)

Legs:
Shift the weight forward to the left leg so the weight is more evenly distributed between both legs. Rotate the right foot outward 90 degrees. (Image 9.1-9.3)

Torso:
As the hands circle and the right leg rotates outward, rotate the upper body to the right.

9.1 (side view)   9.2 (side view)   9.3 (side view)

9.4   9.5

Arms:
The hands should continue to rotate to form a ball with the left hand on top (Image 9.4-9.5).

Legs:
Place the weight on the right leg as the body rotates weight, then bring the left foot back together with the right foot (Image 9.4-9.5).

Torso:
The body should now be facing forward (starting direction) after having rotated right with the ball (Image 9.4-9.5).

Block & Punch:
Arms:
Begin by rotating the left hand to point downward while making a fist. The rotation of the arm should be caused by the shoulder rotating forward and down as the elbow raises. Right hand will come from the bottom of the ball to the right hip while forming a fist (Image 9.6).

Legs:
As the left arm rotates, shift the weight onto the right leg and begin to step to the left side with the left foot (Image 9.6).

9.6

9.6 (side view)

Torso:
The torso rotates to the right and slightly downward as the weight shifts more onto the right leg (Image 9.6).

Arms:
During this twisting of the body the left arm starts to block forward by raising and swinging the forearm. The shoulder will begin to rotate back to a relaxed position. The right fist will begin to come forward from the hip, remaining close to the chest. (Image 9.7)

Legs:
Shifting the weight forward onto the left leg through a balanced transitional stance similar to Horse stance (Image 9.7).

9.7

9.7 (side view)

Torso:
Begin rotating the upper torso toward the left (Image 9.7).

9.8

9.8 (side view)

Arms:
As the body twists to face the left hand side the left shoulder will rotate back to a neutral and relaxed position. The left arm will now finish at shoulder height with the entire arm being horizontal. The right fist will continue upward, rotating from palm up to palm down, and straight forward to just below the left arm (Image 9.8).

Legs:
Continue shifted the weight forward towards the left leg until the feet are in a Bow stance (Image 9.8).

Torso:
Continue twisting and rotating the upper body so that the hips and shoulders are facing the left (Image 9.8).

小擒拿手 Catch and hold the hand

Chinese name: 小擒拿手
Pinyin: xiǎo qín ná shǒu
Translation: Small seize, grasp hand
Other names: Small catch and hold the hand

The name of this movement simply describes the relatively small hand movements needed to apply a "qin na" (sometimes chin na) technique, to catch and hold or sometimes referred to as seize and hold often resulting in joint locks and manipulation.

Beginning from the position at the end of Step forward, parry, block, and punch (Image 9.9):

10.1

10.2

Arms:
Begin by rolling both arms down and inward towards the abdomen and chest (Image 10.1-10.2).

Legs:
As the hand roll back towards the chest shift the weight back onto the right leg (Image 10.2). After the weight has been shifted, turn the left foot outward to the left (Image 10.2) and begin shifting the weight forward onto the left leg (Image 10.3).

Torso:
The hips and shoulders will remain facing to the left and only move minimally and naturally (Image 10.1-10.3).

10.1 (side view)

10.2 (side view)

10.3

10.4

Arms:
The right hand leads by unrolling in a vertical circle upward and forward. The left hand follows the same kind of path. The path of the left hand is a much smaller radius made using more of the wrist to arc out (Image 10.2-10.3). The hands then simultaneously grasp forward (Image 10.3-10.4).

Legs:
The weight is then almost completely shifted onto the left leg and the right leg begins to bend at the knee and start moving forward (Image 10.3-10.4).

Torso:
The torso then completes rotating to the left stopping at 90 degrees left of starting direction (Image 10.3-10.4).

10.3 (side view)

10.4 (side view)

141

右踢腿 Right kick

Chinese name: 右踢腿
Pinyin: yòu tī tuǐ
Translation: Right kick
Other names: Right ridge kick

Although having the general name of right kick, this movement uses a very specific type of kick known as a ridge kick. This kick turns the leg inward at the hip and extends at the knee while keeping the foot flexed so that the main striking area is the outside edge the right foot. As the foot extends outward the arms pull in towards the body slightly.

11.1   11.1 (side view)

Arms:
The arms stay relatively stationary only beginning to move in towards the body.

Legs:
All the weight sinks into the left leg as the right leg is raised bending at the knee with the right foot staying roughly in front of the left knee (Images 11.1).

Torso:
The hips, shoulders and chest all remain facing to the left.

11.2   11.2 (side view)

Arms:
Both arms pull in towards the body to the left staying equidistant apart (Images 11.2).

Legs:
The right leg extends forward striking with the ridge of the foot (Images 11.2).

左打虎式 Hit the tiger – left side

> Chinese name: 左打虎式
> Pinyin: zuǒ dǎ hǔ shǐ
> Translation: Left striking tiger
> Other names: Strike the tiger -left side

This move involves circling the left hand from inside to outward with a closed fist, striking around with a left hook at head height, "striking the tiger." Several moves in Wudang Zhang Sanfeng tai chi have names involving striking tigers, many of which use circular or hooking punches. (e.g. Embracing the tiger and Draw bow and shoot Tiger).

From Right kick close both hands to form lightly clenched fists (Images 12.1).

| 12.1 | 12.2 | 12.3 |

Arms:
The left arm swings like a pendulum down across the front of the body circling outward towards the left hip (Images 12.1-12.2), then continues moving along the same circle back up toward shoulder height (Image 12.3). The right arm bends inward becoming vertical, with the right hand just below eye level, and crossing in front of the torso toward the left (Images 12.1-12.2), continuing to circle downward toward the right hip (Image 12.3).

Legs:
The right leg, after kicking forward steps back behind the left leg at a 45 degree angle (Images 12.1-12.2). After the right leg is firmly on the ground, shift the weight onto it and step the left foot back at a slight angle from the right (Image 12.3)

| 12.1 (side view) | 12.2 (side view) | 12.3 (side view) |

Torso:

The whole body twists to the left being led by the upper body twisting first as an extension of the arm movements (Images 12.2-12.3).

12.4

12.5

12.6

Arms:

The left arm continues its outward arc upward (Images 12.3-12.4). At about half way up the left arm bends at the elbow and the circular motion is completed by the forearm and wrist curving inward at head height (Images 12.5-12.6). The right continues to arc back upward from the right hip and passes in front of the shoulders before swinging downward hinging at the elbow, blocking straight downward in front of the lower body (Images 12.3-12.6).

12.4 (side view)

Legs:

While rotating, shift the weight equally onto both legs (Images 12.4-12.4). As the movement is completed continue by shifting the weight forward towards the left leg into a Bow stance (Images 12.5-12.6).

12.6 (side view)

Torso:
The upper body twists towards the left adding power and momentum to the circles made by both arms resting with hips, chest and shoulders facing the direction the left foot is facing. The body weight also shifts forward in the direction of the left foot.

The final position of this movement is with the left hand striking the "tiger" in the head while than right hand protects the torso. This move is then repeated on the right side.

右打虎式 Hit the tiger – right side

Chinese name: 右打虎式
Pinyin: yòu dǎ hǔ shiǐ
Translation: Right striking tiger
Other names: Strike the Tiger -Right side

This move is a mirror opposite of the last move after first transitioning to face the other direction. The end of this move involves turning the body to face the other direction and receding slightly before circling the right hand from inside to outward with a closed fist, striking around with a right hook at head height.

Transition from doing this move on the other side.

13.1   13.2   13.3

Arms:
The right arm sweeps upward toward the right while the left arms sweeps downward to the left (Images 13.1-13.3), creating a splitting action.

Legs:
The body weight shifts from the left leg back into the right leg creating a Bow stance in the opposite direction (Images 13.1-13.3). Allow the feet to naturally turn on the heels to point to the right.

Torso:
The whole body together rotates to the left a full 180 degrees (Images 13.1-13.3).

13.1 (side view)   13.2 (side view)   13.3 (side view)

13.4

13.5

13.6

Arms:
The right arm swings like a pendulum down across the front of the body circling outward towards the right hip. The left arm bends inward becoming vertical, with the left hand just below eye level, and crossing in front of the torso toward the right (Images 13.4-13.6).

Legs:
The right leg comes back to left leg then steps forward toward the right. During that movement the majority of the weight will be on the left leg (Images 13.4-13.6).

Torso:
The upper body will begin twisting and rotating to the right.

13.4 (side view)

13.5 (side view)

13.6 (side view)

13.7

Arms:
The right arm continues its outward arc upward. At about half way up the right arm bends at the elbow and the circular motion is completed by the forearm and wrist curving inward at head height. The left hand swings downward hinging at the elbow, blocking straight downward in front of the lower body. (Images 13.7-13.8)

13.7 (side view)

Legs:
While rotating, shift the weight equally onto both legs. As the movement is completed continue by shifting the weight forward towards the right leg into a Bow stance. (Images 13.7-13.8)

13.8

Torso:
The upper body twists towards the right adding power and momentum to the circles made by both arms resting with hips, chest and shoulders facing the direction the right foot is facing. The body weight also shifts forward in the direction of the right foot. (Images 13.7-13.8)

左搂膝拗步 Brush the knee and twist-left

Chinese name: 左楼膝拗步
Pinyin: zuǒ lóu xī ǎo bù
Translation: Left brush knee twist step (stance)
Other names: Brush knee, left brush knee

This move is the same as movement number 7, except that this time the starting position has changed and the direction the body will be facing is different.

Video supplements of each individual move and the form in its entirety can be found on you tube by searching for the name of each move and Wudang tai chi or under the user Wudang Yogi.

Links to these YouTube videos can also be found at wesleychaplin.com/videos

14.1

14.2

14.3

Arms:
From the ending position of Hit the Tiger, the right arm will sweep across the chest before (Images 14.2) arcing down across the left side of the body (Images 14.3) to form the bottom part of the ball (Images 14.4 - 14.5). As the right hand begins to fall the left hand finishes its arc upward (Images 14.4 - 14.5) to form the top of the ball (Images 14.6).

Legs:
The weight of the body will shift back onto the left leg (Images 14.2 - 14.3, while the right leg and foot will turn outward to the right (Images 14.2 - 14.4). The weight is then shifted onto the right leg (Images 14.4 - 14.6) and as the hands begin to form the ball the left leg should step together with right leg (Images 14.6).

Torso:
The body will rotate with the formation of the ball to the right about 90 degrees (Images 14.2-14.6).

14.4

14.5

14.6

153

14.7

14.8

Arms:
The left hand sweeps across the chest and arcs down (Images 14.7), falling to the side, arcing forward and outward brushing past the left knee (Images 14.8-14.10). The right hand simultaneously comes to chest level and then pushes straight forward (Images 14.7-14.10).

Legs:
Standing with feet together, step forward to the left slightly with the left leg while keeping the majority of the weight on the right leg (Images 14.7). Shift the weight forward onto the left leg coming into a Bow stance (Images 14.8-14.10).

Torso:
Rotate the upper body to face the direction you are stepping (Images 14.7-14.10). The body rotates slightly to the left to square up in the direction forward (Images 14.10).

14.9

14.10

野马分鬃 Part the wild horse mane

Chinese name: 左楼膝拗步
Pinyin: zuǒ lóu xī ǎo bù
Translation: Left brush knee twist step (stance)
Other names: Brush knee, left brush knee

One of the most common movements, Parting the (wild) horse's mane, is practiced in nearly every style of tai chi. As a result of its common nature and inclusion in many styles, the way the complete movement, parting the horse's mane can look vastly different depending on the practitioner, especially the transition from left to right and back. It is the subtle complexity of the movement that results in its enduring practice through the variety of styles over the centuries.

After brush knee, the right leg is brought to the left leg and the hands form a ball with the right hand bottom (Image 15.1-15.3).

15.1

15.2

15.3

Arms:
Begin by standing with both hands in a ball position with the right hand on the bottom (Image 15.3). Keeping the right arm in the same arched rounded position raise it horizontally to shoulder level. As the right arm rises, push forward with the left hand (Image 15.4 – 15.6).

Legs:
Sinking the weight onto the left leg and moving the right leg forward (Image 15.4 -15.5). Continue by exhaling and shifting the weight forward onto the right leg into a Bow stance (Image 15.4-15.6).

Torso:
The body weight and center of gravity will lower and the body will start rotating to the right (Image 15.4 -15.5).

15.4

15.5

15.6

Arms:

Drawing the right arm back and towards the chest, while the left hand rotates upward and forward (Image 15.7-15.8). During this initial movement the hands and the wrists will also rotate causing the palms to face opposite directions towards each other. The right palm should be mostly facing forward, away from the body, while the left palm faces towards the body.

Legs:

Initially the weight is shifted forward slightly onto the right leg, while adjusting the left leg, before shifting back onto the left leg (Image 15.7-15.8).

15.7

15.8

Arms:

The right hand will continue in a circular motion towards the hip and then begin circling back upward as the left hand rotates forward and up eventually curving back towards the body (Image 15.9 – 15.10).

Legs:

At the beginning of the movement the weight is still moving towards the back, left leg, but as the movement continues the weight begins to be shifted back forward onto the right leg (Image 15.9 – 15.10).

15.7

15.8

Torso:

The body rotates slightly during this movement, but still remains facing forward towards the direction the right foot is pointing (Image 15.9 - 15.13).

15.11   15.12

Arms:
Allow the right hand to follow its natural circular path forward
and up to shoulder height making the top of the ball, while the left
hand circles downward along the side of the body creating the
bottom of the ball (Image 15.11-15.13).

Legs:
The weight is completely shifted onto the right leg, which may
turn slightly out to the right. As the weight is shifted, the left leg
steps forward together with the right leg (Image 15.11-15.12).

Torso:
The upper body follows the arm movement and rotates to the
right, slightly twisting ahead of the lower body. Together the
whole body turns to squarely face the right (Image 15.11-15.12).

This movement which can be a complex set of hand movements
can be aided in trying to remember to keep the hands about equal
distance apart throughout the movement and palms almost facing
each other. To get a feel for this try the Ball exercise in the
Foundations section.

This move is then repeated two more times, first by doing the
movement on the opposite (left) side and then once again to the
right side.

Left side:

15.13   15.14   15.15

Arms:
Begin by standing with a ball right hand on the bottom Keeping
the left arm in the same arched rounded position raise it
horizontally to shoulder level. As the left arm rises, push forward
with the right hand (Image 15.13 – 15.15).

Legs:
Sinking the weight onto the right leg and moving the left leg
forward. Continue by exhaling and shifting the weight forward
onto the right leg into a Bow stance (Image 15.13 – 15.15).

Torso:
The body weight and center of gravity will lower and the body
will start rotating to the left (Image 15.14). Rotate the shoulders
and hips forward in the direction of the knee.

Arms:

Draw the left arm back and towards the chest while the right hand rotates upward and forward (Image 15.16 - 15.17). During this initial movement the hands and the wrists will also rotate causing the palm to face

15.16

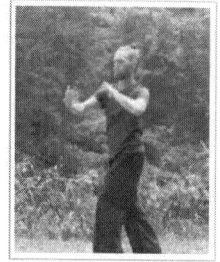

15.17

opposite directions towards each other. The left palm should be mostly facing forward away from the body while the right palm faces towards the body (Image 15.17).

Legs: Initially the weight is shifted forward slightly onto the right leg, while adjusting the left leg, before shifting back onto the left leg (Image 15.16-15.17).

15.18

15.19

15.20

Arms:

The left hand will continue in a circular motion towards the body and scooping downwards as the right hand rotates forward and up eventually curving back towards the body (Image 15.19).

Legs:

At the beginning of the movement the weight is still moving towards the back, right leg, but as the movement continues the weight begins to be shifted back forward onto the left leg (Image 15.18-15.20).

Torso:
The body rotates during this movement but still remains mostly facing forward in the direction the left foot is pointing (Image 15.18 - 15.20).

Arms:
Allow the left hand to follow its natural circular path forward and up to shoulder height making the top of the ball, while the right hand circles downward along the side of the body creating the bottom of the ball (Image 15.21).

15.21

Legs:
The weight is completely shifted onto the left leg, which may turn slightly out to the left. As the weight is shifted the right leg steps forward together with the left leg (Image 15.21).

Torso:
The upper body follows the arm movement and rotates to the left, slightly twisting ahead of the lower body. Together the whole body turns to squarely face the left (Image 15.21). Begin by standing with a ball right hand on the bottom. Sinking the weight and moving the right leg forward while inhaling.

After completing the left side continue by parting the horses mane to the right again, finishing with the feet together and a ball with the left hand on the bottom.

15.23   15.24   15.25

Arms:
Begin by standing with a ball right hand on the bottom (Image 15.22 - 15.23). Keeping the right arm in the same arched rounded position, raise it horizontally to shoulder level. As the right arm rises, push forward with the left hand (Image 15.24 - 15.25).

Legs:
Sinking the weight onto the left leg and moving the right leg forward (Image 15.23). Continue by exhaling and shifting the weight forward onto the right leg into a Bow stance (Image 15.25).

Torso:
The body weight and center of gravity will lower and the body will start rotating to the right (Image 15.23). Rotate the shoulders and hips forward in the direction of the knee.

Arms:
Drawing the right arm back and towards the chest before circling down towards the hip, while the left hand rotates upward and forward (Image 15.26-15.27). During this initial movement the hands and wrists will also rotate causing the palm to face opposite directions towards each other. The right palm should be mostly facing forward away from the body while the left palm faces towards the body.

Legs:
Initially the weight is shifted forward slightly onto the right leg, while adjusting the left leg, before shifting back onto the left leg (Image 15.26-15.27).

15.26   15.27

Arms:
The right hand will continue in a circular motion towards the body and scooping downwards as the left hand rotates forward and up eventually curving back towards the body (Image 15.26 – 15.27).

Legs:
At the beginning of the movement the weight is still moving towards the back, left leg, but as the movement continues the weight begins to be shifted back forward onto the right leg (Image 15.27 – 15.28).

Torso:

The body rotates slightly during this movement but still remains primarily facing forward towards the direction of the right foot is pointing (Image 15.27 – 15.29).

15.28   15.29   15.30

Arms:

Allow the right hand to follow its natural circular path forward and up to shoulder height making the top of the ball, while the left hand circles downward along the side of the body creating the bottom of the ball (Image 15.28 – 15.30).

Legs:

The weight is completely shifted onto the right leg, which may turn slightly out to the right. As the weight is shifted the left leg steps forward together with the right leg (Image 15.29 – 15.30).

Torso:

The upper body follows the arm movement and rotates to the right, slightly twisting ahead of the lower body. Together the whole body turns to squarely face the right (Image 15.29 - 15.30). That is the end of the actual movement of parting the horse's mane, there is a final move that acts as a transition into the next movement, single whip.

15.31   15.32   15.33

Arms:
Both the left and right hand circle initially towards the right hip (Image 15.31), the hands then circle and to the left as the body rotates in that direction (Images 15.32-15.33). Face both palms outward to the left, rotating at the waist while bringing both hands across the chest.

Legs:
As the body moves forward the left leg is lifted, bending at the knee, up to waist height (Images 15.31-15.32), the left foot then extends forward to about knee height and the left leg straightens. the left foot should be turned outward and just below knee height (Images 15.32-15.33).

Torso:
The body moves forward, while the shoulders and hips turn left (Images 15.31-15.33).

15.34　　　　　　　15.35　　　　　　　15.36

Arms:
Both hands finish coming across the chest and continue circling down to the hips. Once the hands reach the right hip, the fingers of the right hand come together to form a crane beak similar to at the end of Grasp the sparrow's tail (Images 15.34-15.37).The left hand relaxes with fingers extended and is placed just below the elbow.

Legs:
The left leg will step forward and turn outward and come to the ground as the hands finish crossing the body. he weight is shifted to the right leg and left leg steps back together with the right.

15.37

正单鞭 Straight single whip

Chinese name: 正单鞭
Pinyin: zhèng dān biān
Translation: Straight single whip
Other names:

This version of single whip is much more simplified than the first time around; in fact the way it is practiced here is in its most simple form, it contains no kick or repetition.

See movement 4 for a more detailed explanation. It is only the movement of bringing the left arm from the right shoulder across the chest to the left, while shifting to the left.

16.1

16.2

16.3

Arms:
The left hand will start to cross the chest and the right hand will slightly relax, while the waist will begin to rotate to the left. The left hand will sweep across the front of the body continuing to extend forward (Image 16.2-16.4).

Legs:
Begin by stepping to the left, preparing for shifting into a Bow stance. Continue with the left foot shifting the weight forward to a Bow stance (Image 16.2-16.4).

Torso:
While shifting forward remember to rotate the waist and hips so that they face left (Image 16.2-16.4).

The movement should coordinate to get the feeling of a whip like motion from the right foot transferring to the arm extending forward striking with the ridge of the hand.

16.4

168

玉女穿梭 Jade woman works the shuttles

Chinese name: 玉女穿梭
Pinyin: yù nǚ chuān suō
Translation: Jade woman shuttles
Other names: Fair woman shuttles around, Young lady works at shuttles

This movement is commonly found in many forms and styles of tai chi and is translated into a variety of names. Most often the name references a woman or girl working at or the shuttles. Shuttles refers to the action of shuttling back and forth of the woman. A unique quality in this movement is the practice of completely changing direction by rotating and spinning the body during the transitions.

Beginning from the single whip position (Image 17.1):

17.1   17.2   17.3

Arms:
The left hand drops down and circles to form the bottom of the ball and the right hand comes up to form the top of the ball (Image 17.1-17.3). The hands stay in this position holding the ball while the body rotates to the right. (Images 17.4-17.6)

Legs:
The weight is shifted back onto the right leg as it turns to the right. As the upper body makes its rotation to the right, the left leg comes forward to the right leg (Image 17.3-17.6)

Torso:
The body will begin by rotating at the waist and continue to rotate to the right with hips, chest, and shoulders (Image 17.3-17.5).

17.4   17.5   17.6

This is the actual starting position of the movements that give this movement its name (Image 17.5), everything before is just the transition from straight Single Whip to Jade Woman Shuttles.

17.7   17.8

Arms:
Bring the left arm upward and slightly rotate it outward as the right arm pushes forward at chest level with the palm facing forward (Image 17.7-17.8). *Notice the left arm will be slightly vertical and turned out to the left.

Legs:
Step forward at a 45 degree angle with the left leg, shifting the weight forward onto the left leg in Bow stance (Image 17.7-17.8).

Torso:
The entire body rotates to face the direction of the left foot (Image 17.7-17.8).

At this point the body is going to rotate 180 degrees to face the opposite direction, this rotation is achieved by twisting at the waist, rotating the hips to face that direction, and the feet will rotate in that direction as well. *Remember when turning to try and keep as much of the foot in contact with the ground, maintaining as stable a root as possible, rotating on the heels.

Arms:
The right hand begins by following a large circular path upward and to the right, while the left arm falls and circles inward towards the left hip (Image 17.9-17.10).

Legs:
Both the left and right feet turn a 180 degrees to the right on the heels of the feet. Shift the weight back onto the right foot as the left toes are raised and the left foot turns 180 degrees (Image 17.10). Then shift the weight more onto the left leg as the right foot turns (Image 17.11).

17.9

17.10

Torso:
The upper body will rotate with the legs rotation (Image 17.10-17.11).

Arms:
The right arm continues to circle out and to the right finishing at the bottom of the ball, as the left hand circles upward and outside on the left finishing by making the top of the ball (Image 17.11-7.12).

Legs:
The right leg will be brought back together with the left foot (Image 17.12).

17.11

17.12

Torso:
The body follows the rotation of the legs movements so as to not twist (Image 17.12).

At this point you should be standing mostly on the left leg, holding a ball with the left hand on top and traveled to face approximately 270 degrees to the right of the start of this move (Image 17.12).

17.13

17.14

17.15

Arms:
Bring the right arm upward and slightly rotate it outward as the left arm and palm pushes forward at chest level (Image 17.13 - 17.14). *Notice the left arm will be slightly vertical and turned out to the left.

Legs:
Step forward at a 45 degree angle with the right leg, shifting the weight forward onto the right leg in Bow stance (Image 17.13 - 17.14).

Torso:
The entire body rotates to face the direction of the right foot (Image 17.13 -17.14).

17.16   17.17   17.18   17.19

Arms:
Keeping the left arm at chest level drawing it in close, while the right arm sweeps downward towards the center of the body and then outward. The left arm then circles down and around to form the bottom of the ball, while the right hand circles up and outward to form the top of the ball. (Images 17.16-17.19)

Legs:
The weight is slightly shifted back onto the left leg before shifting all the weight forward onto the right leg. Shift the weight forward and step the left leg to the right (Images 17.16-17.19).

Torso:
The body begins by rotating to the right, then rotates back left while stepping forward and the right hand begin going upward.

At this point the complete movement is now repeated again. The difference between the first set and this set are their respective starting and ending points, this results in the movement being done facing the opposite direction. By doing the movement twice the movement is able to finish where it began.

Arms:
Bring the left arm upward and slightly rotate it outward as the right arm pushes forward at chest level with the palm facing forward (Image 17.20-17.23). *Notice the left arm will be slightly vertical and turned out to the left.

17.20

Legs:
Step forward at a 45 degree angle with the left leg, shifting the weight forward onto the left in Bow stance (Image 17.20-17.23).

Torso:
The entire body rotates to face the direction of the left foot (Image 17.20-17.23).

17.21

17.22

17.23

The body then rotates 180 degrees to face the opposite direction, this rotation is achieved by twisting at the waist, rotating the hips to face that direction, and the feet will rotate in that direction as well. *Remember when turning to try and keep as much of the foot in contact with ground maintaining as stable a root as possible, rotating on the heels.

17.24   17.25   17.26

Arms:
The right hand begins by following a large circular path upward and to the right, while the left arm falls and circles inward towards the left hip (Image 17.24-17.26).

Legs:
Both the left and right feet turn a 180 degrees right on the heels of the feet. Shift the weight back onto the right foot as the left foot turns 180 degrees (Image 17.26). Then shift the weight more onto the left leg as the right foot turns (Image 17.27).

Torso:
The upper body will rotate with the legs rotation (Image 17.24-17.29).

17.27   17.28   17.29

176

Arms:

The right arm continues to circle out and to the right finishing at the bottom of the ball, as the left hand circles upward and outside on the left finishing by making the top of the ball (Image 17.27-7.29).

Legs:

The right leg will be brought back together with the left foot (Image 17.29).

17.30   17.31   17.32

Arms: Bring the right arm upward and slightly rotate it outward as the left arm and palm pushes forward at chest level (Image 17.30 -17.32). *Notice the left arm will be slightly vertical and turned out to the left.

Legs: Step forward at a 45 degree angle with the right leg, shifting the weight forward onto the right in Bow stance (Image 17.30 -17.32).

Torso: The entire body rotates to face the direction of the right foot (Image 17.30 -17.32).

17.33   17.34   17.35

Arms:
Both the left and right hands will circle slightly outward to the right as the arms begin to lower and circle in towards the left hip (Image 17.33 -17.35).

Legs:
As the hands circle towards the hips the weight of the body is shifted from the right leg in front back onto the left leg (Image 17.33 -17.35).

Torso:
The body which was leaning slightly forward on the right side will come back so that the shoulders and hips are both facing forward as the hands approach the hips (Image 17.33 -17.35).

17.36   17.37   17.38

Arms: Both arms continue in a circle towards the right hip and upward. As the arms rise to chest level they circle back to the left in conjunction with the extension of the left leg (Image 17.36 - 17.38).

Legs: Once the hands reach the hips the weight of the body moves forward onto the right leg. As the body continues forward the left leg is extended at a 45 degree angle from the forward movement, with the foot at about knee height (Image 17.36 - 17.38).

Torso: Initially the body moves forward with the hips and shoulders facing forward, as the left leg is extended the hips and torso turn to left (Image 17.36 -17.38).

| 17.39 | 17.40 | 17.41 |

Arms: The hands continue their circular movement to the left down toward the left hip (Image 17.39 -17.41).

Legs: The left foot is placed on the ground while the weight of the body is shifted onto it. In this position the left leg will be crossed in front of the right leg (Image 17.39 -17.41).

Torso: The torso continues to rotate to the left until it is 90 degrees from the beginning of transition (Image 17.39 -17.41).

| 17.42 | 17.43 | 17.44 |

Arms:
Once the arms reach the level of the hips raise them laterally on the right side (Image 17.42). The right arm rises slightly before the left arm and is extended with the right arm bent. The left arm follows slightly below with the left hand following the right elbow. As the right arm reaches shoulder height the fingers of the right hand come together to form a "crane beak," same as the end of grasp the sparrow's tail (Image 17.43 -17.44).

Legs:
The weight is fully shifted onto the left leg, while the right leg follows and is placed next to the left leg. As the legs come together the weight is evenly distributed between them (Image 17.42 -17.44).

This movement can be practiced continuously in a small space because of the movements' symmetrical and repetitious pattern. The movement creates a diamond pattern if repeated once the end position should be the same as the starting position. The form can be practiced continuously by repeating the moves from at Image 17.4 to 17.35. This is a more complex movement but can be beneficial to be practiced in a fashion similar to the foundation exercises. Practice of this movement can greatly help the understanding of changing directions, larger circular movements, and helps in fluidity overall.

正单鞭 Straight single whip

Chinese name: 正单鞭
Pinyin: zhèng dān biān
Translation: Straight single whip
Other names:

This version of single whip is done in the same way as it was done two moves ago, movement 16, in the most simplified way.

18.1

18.2

Arms:
The left hand will start to cross the chest and the right hand will slightly relax, while the waist will begin to rotate to the left. The left hand will sweep across the front of the body continuing to extend forward (Image 18.1 – 18.5).

Legs:
Begin by stepping to the left, preparing for shifting into a Bow stance. Continue with the left foot shifting the weight forward to a Bow stance (Image 18.1 – 18.5).

Torso:
While shifting forward remember to rotate the waist and hips so that they face left (Image 18.1 - 18.5).

18.3

18.4

18.5

The movement should coordinate to get the feeling of a whip like motion from the right foot transferring to the arm extending forward striking with the ridge of the hand.

蛇身下势 Push down

Snake creeps down is often known simply as Push down because of the way the body drops down toward the ground. The body is then kept close to the ground as the weight shifts forward and then upward at the very end. This move requires a lot of practice and flexibility in drop stance to do properly. This move can also be practiced by keeping the torso and body weight higher. The body should only go as low in the drop stance while still being able to keep both feet completely on the ground and the body balanced.

| 19.1 | 19.2 | 19.3 | 19.4 |

Arms:
Bring the left hand across the body in a circular movement toward the right shoulder (Image 19.2 – 19.4).

Legs:
The weight is shifted more back onto the right leg as the left foot turns inward, right (Image 19.2 – 19.4).

Torso:
The upper body will rotate to square the hips and shoulders forward with the feet (Image 19.2 – 19.4).

19.5   19.6   19.7   19.8

Arms:
The left arm continues its circle downward along the right side of the body (Image 19.5-19.7).

Legs:
Using the mostly the right leg to support the body weight lower down allowing the left leg to slide forward along the ground if comfortable (Image 19.5-19.7). **The right heel should remain on the ground at all times, if it is not slowly work up the flexibility to do so.

Torso:
The body should remain relatively straight while lowering down. Do not bend over or curve the back to try and get lower to the ground. If very flexible and low to the ground, then the upper body can be lowered by bending at the waist.

19.5c   19.6c   19.7c   19.8c

186

Variations:
A key difficulty in this one is the ability to lower the body all the way to the ground. The flexibility and strength to get to the final stage can be built up in a number of ways. In the form and while moving the modified version involves lowering to the most comfortable level where the foot is flat on the ground and the spine is staying relatively straight (not leaning forward). Images 19.5c -19.8c are an example of performing the movement at a higher level.

Arms:
The left arm stay facing forward slightly bent at the elbow with the fingers pointing upward.(Image 19.6-19.10). The right arm rotates at the shoulder, elbow, and wrist rotate towards the right hip with the fingers stay together in a crane formation with the finger tips facing upward.

Legs:
The placement of the legs stay the same, but the body is shifted forward until the majority of the weight is on the left foot. (Images 19.9-19.10) The final position of the legs should be in a Bow stance facing to the left.

Torso:
As the body weight shifts forward the body also raises up while the shoulders and hips square left with the feet.(Image 19.9 - 19.10)

19.9

19.10

上步七星 Step forward with seven stars

Seven stars refers to the large seven stars that make up the big dipper and in Chinese traditional culture, philosophy, martial arts, etc. it is commonly referenced and viewed as important and auspicious. This move is named so because from a certain angle the body position looks similar to that of the large dipper.

Arms:
The left arm will lead forward curving upward with the shoulder while bending at the elbow (Image 20.2).

Legs:
The weight is shifted forward onto the left leg, as this happens the left knee will bend and the right leg will straighten as the weight continues forward and up (Image 20.2).

Torso:
The torso will begin to twist slightly to the left as the body moves forward and up (Image 20.2).

20.1   20.2   20.3

Arms:
While coming forward bend the left arm at the elbow and rotate the arm to cross in front of the chest. The right hand will simultaneously circle down to the right hip (Image 20.2-20.3).

Legs:
Continue shifting the weight forward completely onto the left leg (Image 20.2-20.3).

Torso:
The torso remains facing forward and square (Image 20.2-20.3).

Arms:
As the exhalation is completed the left arm, remaining horizontal, and hand continues to move closer to the chest while the right fist comes forward and up from the hip (Image 20.4-20.5).

Legs:
The right leg will come forward and kick with the inside arch at shin level (about a foot) (Image 20.4-20.5).

Torso:
Stationary, forward facing (Image 20.4-20.5).

20.4   20.5

Tip:
When coming forward try to keep the right elbow and right knee moving together.

退步跨虎 Step backward and ride the tiger

Chinese name: 退步跨虎
Pinyin: tuì bù kuà hǔ
Translation: Step backward straddling the tiger
Other names:

The name refers to the initial step back, following the last move, into the main placement of the legs throughout. The hands do most of the moving throughout this movement. The hands, like in move 12 and13 Striking the tiger, circle around the outside of the body before circling forward with the back of the fist.

Video supplements of each individual move and the form in its entirety can be found on you tube by searching for the name of each move and Wudang tai chi or under the user Wudang Yogi.

Links to these YouTube videos can also be found at wesleychaplin.com/videos

Coming from the position from move 20 stepping forward with seven stars,

21.1

21.2

Arms:

The right fist will lower to the right hip as the left elbow rotates down towards the navel as the left fist rotates upward and out toward the left shoulder, so the left fist is at head height and arm straight up and down (Image 21.2-21.5).

Legs:

The right leg moves backward to several feet behind and in align with left foot, creating a Bow stance (Image 21.2-21.5).

21.3

21.4

21.5

21.6

21.7

Arms:
The right arm will continue to arc up and outward in a circular motion from the hip finishing at shoulder height. The left hand will sweep across and down the front of the body, circling slightly outward, finishing by circling at the wrist back towards the navel (Image 21.6-21.9).

Legs:
The right foot starts to come to the floor and the center of gravity comes back to a low and stable position (Image 21.6-21.9).

Torso:
Center of gravity comes back and downward rooting in through both feet (Image 21.6-21.9).

The final position at the end of exhalation has the right fist at shoulder level and the left arm at hip level both curved as if encircling something.

21.8

21.9

Right side

This movement is repeated exactly the same on the opposite side, the movement is a mirror of the first half. To make the transition:

| 21.10 | 21.11 | 21.12 |

Arms: The right hand will fall towards the right hip (Image 21.10-21.13) and the left arm comes vertically toward the center line.

Legs: The weight is shifted back onto the right foot as the left foot turns inward to the right (Image 21.10-21.13).

Torso: The rotation is created by turning the entire body including feet, shifting weight towards the right and twist the hips to the front as well (Image 21.10-21.13).

| 21.13 | 21.14 | 21.15 |

Arms: The left arm will sweep across the front of the body just right of the center line as the right arm circles upward (Image 21.13-21.16).

Legs: The weight is now shifted back onto the left leg while the right foot turns outward to the right (Image 21.13-21.16).

21.16

21.17

Arms:
Bring the left hand to the hip from the inside curving outward, while bringing the right arm across the chest vertically just left of the centerline (Image 21.16).

Legs:
At the beginning of this movement the weight should be finishing moving back onto the left leg and begin shifting forward (Image 21.16-21.17).

Arms:
The left arm will circle up from the left hip as the right arm falls to the right hip and circles around at the wrist (Image 21.16-21.18). The left hand should finish at head height curled inward and the right hand should be curled in at navel height (Image 21.19).

21.18

21.19

Legs:
Shift forward onto the right leg and solidify both feet firm into the ground forming a well rooted Bow stance (Image 21.17-21.19).

双摆莲 Wave double lotus kick

Chinese name: 双摆莲
Pinyin: shuāng bǎi lián
Translation: Double (pair) waving lotus
Other names: Double lotus kicks

The double waving lotus kicks is named after the appearance and arc that lotus flowers make when blowing in the wind. In the same way, the legs swing and arc across the body one after the other, beginning with the right leg swinging outward. This movement is not only unique in using relatively quick, high kicks, but it also involves rotating and turning the body a complete 360 degrees on one leg.

22.1   22.2   22.3

Arms:
The right arm rises to shoulder height while remaining turned outward. Both the left and right hands should relax and open so that the palms are facing outward. The arms form a circle with the hands meeting in front of the body between shoulder and eye level. The arms will remain in this position throughout the entire movement. (Image 22.2).

Legs:
The weight is shifted forward onto the right leg As the body weight shifts forward onto the right leg, the left leg swings outward and as it raises the leg the begins to circle to the right, across the front of the body.(Image 22.1-22.6).

Torso:
The body should naturally rotate with the momentum of the kick.

22.4   22.5   22.6

22.7   22.8   22.9

Arms: Remaining in a circular position with the palms facing outward (Image 22.7 – 22.12).

Legs: Both legs should be bent slightly at the knee. Once the left leg begins to cross the front of the body the moment should carry the body to the right, causing the right foot to turn to the right (Image 22.7 - 22.9). Once the body rotates about 90 degrees the left foot should circle down to the ground.

22.10   22.11   22.12

Arms: Remaining in a circular position with palms facing outward (Image 22.10 – 22.12).

Legs: As the left foot finishes it kick across the body it comes to land next to the right foot. As soon as the left foot is on the ground, weight is shifted onto it and the right leg begins to rise up to the left across the body (Image 22.10 - 22.12).

Torso: The body continues rotating right another 90 degrees.

22.13   22.14   22.15

Arms: Remaining in a circular position with the palms facing outward (Image 22.13 – 22.15).

Legs: The right leg continues rising from the left side of the body and circling outward across the body to the right (Image 22.13 - 22.15).The left foot will natural rotate with the momentum of the movement so that it is facing the same direction as the torso.

22.16   22.17   22.18

Arms: Remaining in a circular position with the palms facing outward (Image 22.16 – 22.18).

Legs: The right leg finishing its outside kick by coming to the ground parallel to the left foot at about shoulder width apart (Image 22.16 – 22.18).

Torso: The body continues rotating right another 90 degrees.

弯弓射虎 Bend the bow and shoot the tiger

Chinese name: 弯弓射虎
Pinyin: wān gōng shè hǔ
Translation: Draw bow shoot tiger
Other names: Shoot the tiger

The name of the movement is another fairly descriptive name. The name becomes clear during the first part of the movement when the body sinks down and the arms reach out as if drawing back the string of the bow. The movement continues forward with a circular strike at head height, which represents the shooting of the tiger. This strike, like other movements containing tigers, involves using a circular action and striking with the back of the fist.

Coming from the position after move 22 Double lotus kicks, this move is a direct continuation after the right leg kick. The leg should land in a high horse stance, anywhere from 1.5 to 2.5 times shoulder width apart. After the leg lands on the ground begin to inhale, sinking the weight and keeping yourself centered.

23.1

23.2

23.3

Arms:
Extend the left arm and fist straight out directly left and pull the right arm back keeping it bent and close to the chest (Image 23.2-23.7).

Legs:
The legs stay relatively stationary, only bend at the knees sinking downward (Image 23.2-23.7).

Torso:
As the "bow" is drawn taught, the body should sink and root itself into a Horse stance.

23.4

23.5

23.6

23.7

23.8

23.9

Arms: Relax the right arm flowing down towards the hip in a circular motion; simultaneously the left elbow will relax down towards the navel and the left arm will retract becoming vertical (Image 23.7-23.9).

Legs: Shift the weight back onto the right leg (Image 23.7-23.9)

Torso: As the weight shifts back and the right hand comes to the hip the upper body will twist and rotate the hips to face the left.

23.10

23.11

23.12

Arms: While stepping forward allow the left arm to continue in a circular motion crossing downward in front of the body and the right arm raises circularly up from the outside (Image 23.10-23.12). The right hand should be extended forward at head height and the left hand should extend downward and close to the body.

Legs: Change the shifting of the weight and step forward bringing the right foot forward together with the left foot.

Torso: Stationary forward hips, chest and shoulders.

23.13   23.14

Arms: The right arm relaxes and starts moving downward by becoming horizontal at shoulder height (Image 23.13), while the left arm bends upward close to the body. For this brief moment the hands are in a pseudo ball (Image 23.14-23.15).

Legs: The left leg steps back a short step (Image 23.13-23.14).

Torso: The upper body stays facing forward as it shifts back.

23.15   23.16   23.17

Arms: The left hand rises to guard the right side of the face (Image 23.15-23.217).

Legs: The weight is shifted back completely onto the left leg as the right rises off the ground and up so that right foot is covering the left knee (Image 23.15-23.17).

Torso: The body rotates slightly to the left (Image 23.15-23.17). The final position has just the right side facing forward, while protecting the body with the arms and raised leg.

上步搬拦捶 Step forward, parry, and punch

Chinese name: 上步搬拦捶
Pinyin: shàng bù bān lán chuí
Translation: Step forward, move, block, punch
Other names:

The same movement as done previously in movement 9 is repeated here for the final time. The key difference is that this version begins from a different starting position, but the movements remain the same after the initial turn (Image 24.1-24.3).

Video supplements of each individual move and the form in its entirety can be found on you tube by searching for the name of each move and Wudang tai chi or under the user Wudang Yogi.

Links to these YouTube videos can also be found at wesleychaplin.com/videos

Transition

24.1   24.2   24.3

Arms: Arc the right hand to the right shoulder, then down the right side of the torso while the left hand falls down towards the left hip (Image 24.1-24.3).

Legs: Shift the weight to the left leg and raise the right leg about a foot off the ground while rotating it outward 90 degrees and forward. The right foot turns outward (Image 24.1-24.3).

Torso: As the hands move, rotate the upper body to the right (Image 24.1-24.3).

24.4   24.5   24.6

Arms: The hands should continue to rotate to form a ball with the left hand on top (Image 24.4 – 24.6).

Legs: Place the weight on the right leg as the weight shifts forward, then bring the left foot back together with the right foot. (Image 24.4 - 24.6).

Step forward, Deviate, and Parry:

24.7

24.8

Arms:
Begin by rotating the left hand to point downward while making a fist (Image 24.7). The rotation of the arm should be caused by the shoulder rotating forward and down as the elbow raises (Image 24.7-24.8). Keep the arm bent. Right hand will come from the bottom of the ball to the right hip while forming a fist (Image 24.7).

Legs:
As the left arm rotates, shift the weight onto the right leg and begin to step to the left side (which is forward along center line of form) with the left foot (Image 24.7).

Torso:
The torso will rotate to the right and slightly downward as the weight shifts more onto the right leg (Image 24.7).

Arms:
During this twisting of the body the left arm starts to block forward by raising and swinging up and the forearm. The shoulder will begin to rotate back to a relaxed position. The right fist will begin to come forward from the hip, remaining close to the body (Image 24.9).

24.9

Legs:
Shift the lower weight forward onto the left leg through a balanced transitional stance similar to Horse stance (Image 24.9).

Torso:
Twist and rotate the upper torso toward the left (Image 24.9).

While completing the exhale and twisting motion,

Punch
Arms:
As the body twists to face the left hand side the left shoulder will rotate back to a neutral and relaxed position. The left arm will now finish at shoulder height with the entire arm being horizontal. The right fist will continue upward, rotating from palm up to palm down, and straight forward to just below the left arm (Image 24.10).

24.10

Legs:
Continue shifted the weight forward towards the left leg until the feet are in a Bow stance (Image 24.10).

Torso:
Continue twisting and rotating the upper body so that the hips and shoulders are facing the left (Image 24.10).

如封似闭 Apparent close-up

Chinese name: 如封似闭
Pinyin: rú fēng sì bì
Translation: As if appearing to close up
Other names:

The body placement and movements looks as if closing up, only to perform one last movement, a push, before actually closing up the form. The hands fall downward while the weight shifts back after striking from the last movement, appearing as if receding or finishing. Only after relaxing back then the body rotates while circling that energy back upward and forward through pushing forward with the hands and shifting the weight back forward into a Bow stance.

| 25.1 | 25.2 | 25.3 |

Beginning from after the punch in the last move:

Arms: Allow the hands to relax squaring up with the hips and drawing in toward the chest (Image 25.2 – 25.3).

Legs: Shift the weight mostly back onto the right leg (Image 25.2 - 25.3).

Torso: **Remember when shifting weight back not to lean back.**

| 25.4 | 25.5 | 25.6 |

Arms: The hands cross each other in front of the chest. At the very end of the inhale the hands uncross scooping out and down as if picking something up (Image 25.3 – 25.5).

Legs: With the majority of the weight on the right leg both feet will twist a little to the right (Image 25.3 – 25.4).

Torso: As the weight is shifted back the upper body rotates to the right (Image 25.3 - 25.4).

25.7

25.8

25.9

Arms:
Both arms scoop up to chest level (Image 25.5-25.6) and then push straight forward (Image 25.7 – 25.9)

Legs:
The weight shifts onto the right leg as both feet twist back to the left and then the weight is shifted forward onto the left leg in a Bow stance (Image 25.7 – 25.9).

Torso:
The whole body rotates to the left simultaneously and then remains facing forward on the push out (Image 25.7 - 25.9).

十字手 Cross hands

Chinese name: 十字手
Pinyin: shí zì shŏu
Translation: Ten, word/character, hands
Other names: Cross hands, cross arms

Cross hands is a short movement that describes the position of the arms as the body rotates to face the right side from where originally facing. The arms cross near the hands beginning at the wrist and stay level at around shoulder height. The name refers to the character or written form of the word "ten" (十), which is formed by two lines crossing. In the movement itself the arms cross over each other and resemble the character.

After pushing out at the end of apparent close up:

26.1

26.2

26.3

Arms:
The left arm crosses above the right forearm, creating the position and image for which the move is named (Image 26.1 – 26.2).

Legs:
The weight should be shifted back to the right leg until it is evenly distributed between both legs (Image 26.1 - 26.3). The left foot should then turn inward to the right and come into a Horse Stance (Image 26.4).

Torso:
Rotate the body forward so that both hips and shoulders facing forward (Image 26.1 - 26.4).

The final position after inhalation should feet, knees, hips, shoulders, head, and eyes facing forward. Both arms should be round in front of the chest at just below shoulder height, crossing each other evenly at the forearms, creating the name of the movement.

26.4

抱虎归山 Hold the tiger and return to the mountain

> *Chinese name:* 抱虎归山
> *Pinyin: bào hǔ guī shān*
> *Translation: Embrace the tiger and return to the mountain*
> *Other names:*

The final movement in the form before closing has the body return to the initial relaxed standing position with feet shoulder width apart. This movement involves scooping the arms downward as if picking something heavy up, or "embracing the tiger," and then lifting the hands up above the head together before relaxing the arms down to the side, thus "returning to the mountain."

Arms:
Open both arms
and circle them
downward (Image
27.1 – 27.3).

Legs:
Both legs bend at
the knee, similar
to a squat(Image
27.1 - 27.3).

27.1

27.2

The body is in a position as if to lift something very heavy. The second half of the movement is as if lifting that heavy object and placing it on a shelf at head height.

Arms:
Both arms stay close to the body and circular down to below the waist (Image 27.4 – 27.5).

Legs: Both legs remaining in horse stance bend at the knees pushing outward (Image 27.4 - 27.5). ** Do not allow the knees to buckle inward, this can cause knee injuries**

27.3

27.4

27.5

27.6

27.7

27.8

Arms:
Lift both hands up to head height (Image 27.6 - 27.9), then allow both hands to relax down towards the hips (Image 27.10 – 27.11).

Legs:
Shift the weight to the right leg and move the left leg closer inward so that the legs are between shoulder and hip width apart. Keep a slight bend in the knees (Image 27.7 - 27.11).

27.9

27.10

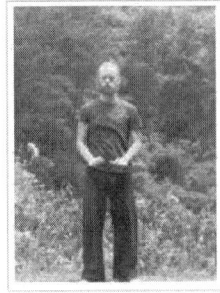

27.11

Final Relaxation
At the end of this move the hands can be placed on the stomach and stand straight. In this position simply focus on breathing through the abdomen with long deep breaths. This is optional. Stay standing and focus on the breath for as long as comfortable but generally not more than 30 minutes. This standing and relaxation can also serve as a meditation in addition to helping to fully relax the body after practice.

215

收势 Finishing

To finish the form, take a deep breath in, relax the arms at the side, exhaling and relaxing step the left foot together with the right foot.

| 28.1 | 28.2 | 28.3 | 28.4 |

Video supplements of each individual move and the form in its entirety can be found on YouTube by searching for the name of each move and Wudang tai chi or under the user Wudang Yogi.

Links to these YouTube videos can also be found at wesleychaplin.com/videos

About the Author

Wesley Chaplin began his studies in Wudang Tai chi more than 15 years ago in China at Grandmaster Zhong Yunlong's school, atop the Wudang Mountains in Hubei Province, in central China. While there he studied under Masters Zhong Xuechao, Zhong Xueyong, and Yuan Xiugang, eventually becoming the first foreign disciple under Master Yuan. During the five years he resided there, Wesley became registered at the Purple Mist Temple (Zi Xiao Gong 紫霄宫) and given the Daoist name Yuan Li Hao (袁理豪). Upon leaving the Wudang Mountains Wesley continued his studies in traditional practices within southern China for another ten years before expanding his knowledge base to include other traditional health practices from throughout Asia. Wesley Chaplin also has a degree in Chinese culture and philosophy from the University of Illinois.

22247426R00123

Printed in Poland
by Amazon Fulfillment
Poland Sp. z o.o., Wrocław